ANTIQUE
NEW ENGLAND
HOMES
AND
BARNS

History, Restoration, and
Reinterpretation

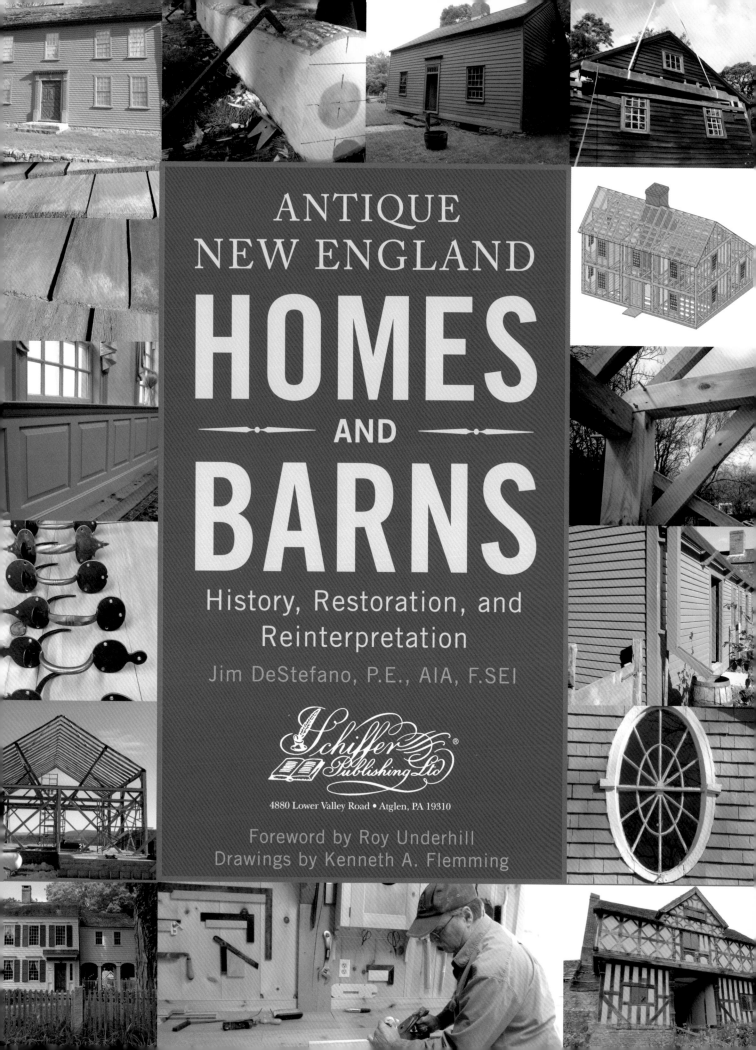

ANTIQUE
NEW ENGLAND
HOMES
AND
BARNS

History, Restoration, and Reinterpretation

Jim DeStefano, P.E., AIA, F.SEI

Schiffer Publishing Ltd.

4880 Lower Valley Road • Atglen, PA 19310

Foreword by Roy Underhill
Drawings by Kenneth A. Flemming

Other Schiffer Books on Related Subjects:

Architectural Details from Old New England Homes,
Stanley Schuler,
ISBN 978-0-7643-0981-6

Old New England Homes, Stanley Schuler,
ISBN 978-0-7643-0995-3

Copyright © 2017 by Jim DeStefano
Foreword copyright by Roy Underhill

Library of Congress Control Number:
2017937433

"Schiffer," "Schiffer Publishing, Ltd.," and the
pen and inkwell logo are registered trademarks
of Schiffer Publishing, Ltd.

Designed by Matt Goodman
Type set in Trade Gothic LT STD & A Caslon

ISBN: 978-0-7643-5353-6
Printed in China

Published by Schiffer Publishing, Ltd.
4880 Lower Valley Road
Atglen, PA 19310
Phone: (610) 593-1777;
Fax: (610) 593-2002
E-mail: Info@schifferbooks.com
Web: www.schifferbooks.com

For our complete selection of fine books on this
and related subjects, please visit our website at
www.schifferbooks.com. You may also write for
a free catalog.

Schiffer Publishing's titles are available at
special discounts for bulk purchases for sales
promotions or premiums. Special editions,
including personalized covers, corporate
imprints, and excerpts, can be created in large
quantities for special needs. For more
information, contact the publisher.

We are always looking for people to write books
on new and related subjects. If you have an
idea for a book, please contact us at
proposals@schifferbooks.com.

This book is dedicated to the one I
love—to my lovely and talented wife,
Vera, whose encouragement, sage
advice, artistry, and legendary home
cooking made this book possible.

CONTENTS

Part One
HISTORY AND EVOLUTION OF THE NEW ENGLAND HOME

Part Two
RESTORATION STRATEGIES

Part Three
BUILDING AND RESTORING

Had I planned this a bit better, I would have connected the replacement drain pipe before installing the heavy support beams in the crawl space. Even before I dragged in the new timbers to support the sagging floor in front of the fireplace, the term crawl space would have been over-generous. Before I set in the beams, I could just reach the smelly cut-off end of the old soil pipe by inchworming over the raw clay beneath the 1910-era floor joists. Now, with the timbers in place, any forward movement requires stunted-nematode-like squirming. So here I am, sandwiched beneath the floor, flashlight held in mouth, both arms forward, one hand holding a screwdriver, the other holding a squeeze bottle of embarrassing personal lubricant that I hope will ease the fit of the reluctant rubber connector needed to mate the end of the new PVC with the gassy end of the old cast iron—and now I see the snake.

He/she is not a stranger. Each building where we live, the Miller's House (above me), the shop, and the Old Mill has its own, very territorial reptile, and this is assuredly his/her territory. Black snakes in particular consider it a point of honor never to back down, even if the spot they are defending is the broken end of a cast iron sewer pipe. So, with progress blocked, I find myself rewarded with the gift of time. Until the snake decides to move on, I have time to contemplate life's mysteries, primarily, what the hell am I doing here?

Clearly, I am here because this is the place of heroes! Yes, there are those who would hire other people to slither under sagging floors and breathe in the vintage sewer gas while being held at bay by surly serpents, but who would Odysseus have been if he had hired someone else to take his epic journey home? Restoration is our adventure! Here we face monsters, temptations, and true tests of our moral fiber!

Consider the floor above me. Every authority says that sagging floors must be jacked up gradually, at about a quarter inch a year. But the three-inch gap between the center of the floor and the string that I stretched from corner to corner dictated a twelve-year job. So, looking around, I figured what's the worst that could happen? Perhaps that quarter inch a year rule is intended to protect plaster walls. But the walls of the Miller's house are lined with tongue and groove beadboard—so every junction, every three inches, has a little bit of give in this all-wood house. So, as all true heroes must

do, I decide that the rules just don't apply to me! Besides, if I didn't jack the timbers up the full three inches pretty quickly, I would not be able to squirm under them and mend the sewer line and would not be here confronting our snake today.

Roy Underhill. *Courtesy of Dr. Gunnar Lucko.*

Every move in restoration is a moral measure. Consider that brick chimney in the kitchen. The mortar had visibly failed on the top course. Easy enough—I just had to climb up the ladder, take off those loose bricks, clean 'em, and stick 'em back together with fresh mortar. But, once that top course was off, I discovered that the course of bricks below was also loose, so off it came, and the next course down as well, and the next. I have punched the tar baby again! Worse (in the moral dimension) the mortar joints seemed slightly stronger as I worked down. So, how far down do I go? When is the mortar "good enough" that I can stop tearing down and start building back up? All the way to the bottom? Halfway down? Do come and look, for my moral measure is plainly graphed in the brickwork bar chart of the (partially) re-laid chimney for all to see and judge.

In restoration work, every such can of worms that you open leads to a nest of squirrels. Removing the brick chimney exposed where the squirrels have been getting in to nest under the kitchen roof. So here was the place to install the squirrel excluder (a wire one-way tunnel), but nesting means that squirrel babies could be left behind. This leads me away from the brickwork and off to researching the social life of squirrel nutkin. It seems that *Sciurus carolinensis* takes a break between litters in mid-December. So the brick repair and the exclusion had to wait until then. Still, the dead of winter will be no time for a lady rodent to have to find a new home. Thus, it's off to the shop to build a proper squirrel-nesting box to place high in the nearest tree. The chimney repair comes to a halt. There are squirrels to house!

This siren song of distractions never stops. "Caulk me!" "Paint me!" "Patch me!" For lesser mortals, this is a negative. For the heroic procrastinator, however, the unending nature of the work is treasure beyond rubies! There is no tough decision, no awkward conversation, no writing deadline that cannot be postponed when there is so much patching and mending to do! I am never out of sight of a spot of damaged beadboard that doesn't need to be levered back into place. Whatever petty problems I have, there is always a nearby window (ah windows!) that urgently needs to have the old putty dug out. So what if that second extended last-chance deadline is approaching? Sorry—hero at work!

We survive these temptations, only to face monsters. I have met them, and I speak not of my patiently defiant black snake, but of a great creature, full fifty feet long and as thick as my thigh, spewing slow, horrific death from its mouth! Sure, it was just a rented blown-in insulation machine, but it almost got me! There I was, deep into the furthest end of the squat labyrinth of vintage trusses in the low attic space over the Mill. The entrance was forty feet behind me when I hit the button on the remote control. The distant machine at the far end of the hose kicked in and began chewing, fluffing, and shooting fiberglass through my end of the long hose at full blast. But that was the remote's last command to the body of the machine. I pounded the stop button, but the great snake would not be stopped. I tried and tried to stop it, but waited just a bit too long. Looking up, I saw the fluff pouring out my end of the hose was quickly filling the attic space from joists to rafters. I struggled backwards through the relentless pink blizzard, blindly digging my way under and over the diagonal braces, still punching desperately at the useless remote control, my cries for help muffled by R-19... R-32... R-56... R-189... R-662.

But now, the comforting glare of the black snake here beneath the floor assures me that somehow I did escape that attic, and that I am not still trapped up there suspended like a fly in cotton candy. The hero makes his escape, and the next adventure cannot be far away! Writer Jean Shep-

herd's father was a used car salesman who considered it immoral to sell a car without a story to go with it. So too with houses. I live in an old timber-framed, water-powered mill that was already on its third set of Bondo fillings when we bought it. Even the proper restoration work I do won't last forever, but perhaps the stories will have a better chance. It's all about the stories. Not everyone can live Odysseus' epic journey home from the wars, battling the Cyclops and the wrath of vengeful gods, but—we can all have our black snakes and sewer pipes, and we're all just finding our way home.

—Roy Underhill

The former Master Housewright for Colonial Williamsburg and creator of the PBS series The Woodwright's Shop, *Underhill recently opened the Woodwright's School in North Carolina where he teaches traditional hand tool woodworking. In 2009 he and his wife moved into an 1870s vintage mill that still has a sign claiming 1850 out front. He takes comfort in being personally designated as midcentury modern.*

Architecture is my delight, and putting up and
pulling down one of my favorite amusements.

—Thomas Jefferson

My story began in the spring of 1981 when I purchased my antique home in Westport, Connecticut. It didn't look much like an antique at the time. Most people described it as a wreck or just a dump, but I could see its potential and it was just what I was looking for. It wasn't my first renovation project but it was the most ambitious.

I had previously renovated what had been my grandparent's 1840s home and my deceased parents' postwar colonial home to prepare them for sale. But these had been primarily cosmetic improvements, merely quick flips. My meager share of the proceeds from those sales was the down payment on my

My antique wreck, 1981.

antique wreck, for which I paid what seemed like an exorbitant sum of $127,000.00.

My antique home was built in 1809 by Delancy Allen, an alleged distant relative of Ethan Allen—the rowdy leader of Vermont's Green Mountain Boys. Many people are surprised to learn that Ethan Allen was never a furniture maker.

The house remained in the Allen family for 120 years. Delancy's son, Issac, became a spec house builder. He subdivided his dad's farm and built dozens of Greek revival and Victorian homes on the property.

In 1930, a young couple purchased the home from the last of the Allen family owners. They built an addition on the house and modernized it with indoor plumbing and central heat. This was the last time anybody spent a nickel on fixing up the place.

When I acquired it, everything was run down, but fortunately, because it had been neglected, all of the old stuff was still there. The historic fabric was intact.

My original plan was to restore the house in a few years,

sell it for a profit, and do it all over again with another house. It seemed like a good idea at the time, but it was not meant to be.

About five years later I sat myself down and had a long talk with myself. I laid down the law. I was insane if I thought that I was going to do this again. The house was finally weathertight and livable. I no longer had to comb plaster dust out of my hair in the morning. I was going to enjoy the house and continue to restore it at a less frantic pace.

I had also made the biggest mistake any real estate developer could make—I had allowed myself to become emotionally attached. It was no longer a real estate deal, it was now my home for life.

By then I had met Vera, the beautiful and talented young woman who was destined to share my life. When she first visited the home she was horrified that the only furniture in the living room was a table saw. My guy friends thought it was cool, but it scared women away. Vera had serious concerns about whether I could be house broken.

My restored antique home.

to start playing golf. I needed to find a diversion for my creative energies.

In 2003 we purchased ninety-one acres in Warren, Connecticut, as a weekend retreat. Warren is a quaint, rural community in the Litchfield hills of northwestern Connecticut. Our property is a magnificent wooded site, crisscrossed with stone walls, bisected by a stream, and with fallow fields that had not been farmed in forty years. The only remnant of a structure was the derelict foundation of a collapsed barn and silo. I now had no shortage of projects to work on in my free time, and the Westport house could take a rest.

It turned out that my site was across the street from what had been the home and studio of the Americana author and painter Eric Sloane, whose writings had inspired me since my youth. I did not know it when I bought the land; it was just one of those karma things.

The Warren site proved to be a much more ambitious undertaking than the restoration of the Westport house. Landscaping and gardening took on a whole new dimension with ninety-one acres. Forests needed management, timber harvested, stumps pulled, a bridge along with a network of roads built, fields cleared and plowed, and rocks pulled from the ground. I developed a real respect for my predecessors who had to do the very same work with teams of oxen rather than hydraulically powered equipment. Finally I was ready to build. The barn came first, for that would house my workshop and shelter my tractors. Next came the house. Since there was no antique house already on the site, I built a new antique New England saltbox with all of the creature comforts and energy efficiency of a modern home, but with the character of an antique.

Over the subsequent decades, restoration proceeded at a relaxed and civilized pace. The building support systems such as roofing, heating, plumbing, and electrical had been tackled in the early years so I could now focus on the more gratifying finish work. Bite-size portions of the house were cordoned off and worked on while we lived in the rest of the house.

In my professional life as a structural engineer and architect, I design homes and buildings for my clients. In my free time I enjoy designing and building for myself. Mastering historic building trades—carpentry, joinery, blacksmithing, and masonry—soon became a passion. My home became a laboratory where I could experiment with new ideas, building techniques, and materials before unleashing them on my unsuspecting clients. If something didn't work, no one but me would be mad.

After every room in the house had been renovated once, I could not stop. I dove right into a second generation of projects, tearing out things that I did in the 1980s and doing them over with better ideas and workmanship. Thirty years ago my carpentry skills were not as polished as they are today and it sometimes pains me to look at my early work. Consequently, the house remained in a constant state of "under construction," which my lovely wife found unsettling.

When I started any new project on the house, Vera would say something like, "now when we finish this project, the house will be done, right?" I found those words very unsettling. What would I do with my free time? I was not about

It is unlikely that I will live long enough to run out of building projects in Warren and, of course, I continue to tinker with my antique Westport home.

So what is my latest project? Writing a book about it all, of course.

Jim DeStefano
Westport, Connecticut

Quintessential New England village, Litchfield, Connecticut.

When I drive through a New England town, my eye is drawn to the rows of white-painted antique homes guarded by white picket fences. There is no mistaking that I am in New England and I know that I am not in Kansas anymore. Antique homes define the landscape of New England. California has the Pacific Ocean and the majestic redwood forests, Colorado has the Rocky Mountains, Florida has palm trees and beaches, the plains states have amber waves of grain, but back in New England the landscape is characterized by its antique homes.

Antique home down on its luck.

But what is an antique home? Not all old houses are antiques, just as not all the pieces of old junk in your grandmother's attic are antiques.

The vast majority of dwellings that were built when America was young were small, crude affairs devoid of craftsmanship, design, or longevity. These homes have long since perished. A few prosperous landowners had the resources to commission a stylish proper house. A small handful of these homes have survived and are today's antiques.

By the mid-nineteenth century, the industrial revolution was in full swing in New England. Young girls were leaving the farm for jobs in mill towns and the men soon followed. Industrialization not only spurred a decline in life on the farm but also changed the way homes were built. Building materials were being manufactured in factories and shipped by rail. Homes were still being assembled on site, but they were no longer entirely handmade with materials harvested from the land. The antique homes described in this book are predominantly the pre-industrial homes built by hand.

A Vanishing Architectural Heritage

New England antique homes are a finite resource. We are not building any more 200-year-old homes, although we have gotten pretty good at building reproductions that can fool the eye, but that is a topic for another chapter. For centuries, antique homes have been lost to a variety of forces both natural and manmade. Despite the efforts of preservationists, we continue to lose antique homes at a steady rate.

William and Martha Gorman on their farm in Newry, Maine, 1919—living the dream. *Courtesy of Bethel Historical Society.*

The most conspicuous examples are those that fall victim to the wrecker's ball or to fire, but neglect is a much bigger villain. Old homes require a lot of maintenance and a proper restoration can be a costly endeavor. When maintenance is deferred for an extended period, water, gravity, and other forces of nature take over and the home soon returns to the earth.

Neglected old homes are undervalued in the real estate market. These unique fixer-upper opportunities are often snatched up by first-time homebuyers with no passion for antique homes and insufficient financial resources to undertake a proper restoration effort. The homes fall victim to renovation projects that strive to make them resemble that new home that the owners could not afford.

Other antique homes are purchased by homeowners who love them to death. It starts out innocently enough. Those drafty old windows are replaced with new insulated windows. Then the old siding with peeling lead paint is replaced with new clapboards. Of course the plaster and lath has to come down to insulate and upgrade the wiring. Next, a few touches are added to make the house look more historic. That dull front door and trim are replaced with a beautiful reproduction Connecticut Valley doorway. Before you know it, there is no original fabric left. It is like the story the old-timer tells of his grandfather's axe—he replaced the head once and the handle twice but it still works as good as new. It is no longer an antique home, but nobody notices the loss.

All older homes evolve with time. If they do not adapt to changing lifestyles, they cannot survive except as museums. The trick is to restore and renovate antique homes to make them energy efficient and comfortable to live in, without losing the elements that give them character and make them special places to live. That is what this book is about.

Take Me Back

Living in a restored antique home can be a special experience. When you walk in the door it can sometimes feel as though you have just stepped back in time. When coping with the stress and pressures in our lives, it is tempting to become nostalgic about simpler times in days gone by. We yearn for the less complicated days before iPhones, automobiles, central air-conditioning, and antibiotics, when the only things our ancestors had to worry about were freezing to death in the winter or starving to death if their crops failed.

Throughout history, there has never been a time when man has not been nostalgic for a simpler time. More than 150 years have passed since Emerson and Thoreau wrote about getting back to a simpler time, before the industrial revolution arrived on the shores of New England.

Of course the reality is that life has always been hard, particularly for the original owners of our antique homes who had to make a living farming in New England. No matter what your trade or profession may have been, you still had to farm your land if you wanted to eat. Even our aristocratic forefathers such as Washington, Jefferson, and Adams considered themselves farmers first and statesmen second. The harsh climate and bony, hardscrabble soils of New England made farming a very hard life.

Modern Living

Architectural fashion and the creature comforts people expect from their home have changed quite a bit in the four centuries since Europeans first built permanent homes in New England. When our antique homes were built, their owners were primarily interested in shelter from the elements.

Today, homebuyers expect indoor plumbing, central heating, air-conditioning, electricity, and kitchen appliances—things that did not exist when our antique homes were built. But that is not all. They also have come to expect things like ten-foot ceilings, three-car garages, large walk-in closets, five bedrooms with private baths, and living rooms with picture windows. It is little wonder that most homebuyers do not give antique homes a second look.

But there is a breed of individuals that seek out antique homes. Maybe it is out of nostalgia, maybe they lust for traditional architecture, or maybe they just find boxy, sheetrock, postwar homes dull and characterless. Whatever the reason, they find owning, restoring, and living in an antique home a thrill of a lifetime.

Just because you bought an antique home does not mean that you have to forgo creature comforts. Old homes do not have to be cold, drafty, and grim. If you plan your restoration project right and read the rest of this book, you just might end up with a comfortable and efficient antique home with character and historic integrity. There is no reason you cannot live the dream.

It is not the strongest of species that survives
... but the one most responsive to change.
—Charles Darwin, 1809

Building traditions are shaped by the building technology of their time. Throughout history, "form follows function" has been the prime driving force in building construction. Style and fashion have been secondary considerations.

European building technology evolved very little in the thousand years prior to the industrial revolution. The tools and techniques that early English settlers brought to the New World in the seventeenth century would have been familiar to tradesmen from the seventh century. When that ancient building tradition came to America it evolved and adapted to the harsh climate, to the vast forests with abundant resources, and to the shortage of skilled labor. Unleashed from the stagnant policies of Old World craft guilds, tradesmen were free to innovate and a culture of Yankee ingenuity emerged.

Within a generation of the establishment of the Plymouth Plantation, buildings in New England no longer closely resembled the buildings left behind in England. A new building tradition emerged that was uniquely American.

Chapter One
EUROPEAN ANCESTORS

We're Americans . . . our forefathers were kicked
out of every decent country in the world.

—Bill Murray, from the motion picture *Stripes*

The early European inhabitants of New England brought with them the medieval building traditions and technologies of the Old World they had left behind. They came predominantly from an area of southeast England know as East Anglia, and it was the regional building traditions of East Anglia that characterized first-period New England homes.

Timber Frame Construction

Timber frame construction has a long tradition in England that dates to the bronze age. The stones at Stonehenge were joined with mortise and tenon joints shaped with bronze chisels, something that no sane stone mason would attempt unless joining timbers with mortise and tenon joints was the only type of construction he knew.

Timber was not plentiful in medieval England. The vast forests that once covered the land had long since been cleared. Oak was the preferred wood for house frames. English oak is a strong, decay-resistant wood species that could be shaped with hand tools when it was green.

The trees that were available were not tall, straight, forest-grown trees, but rather short, fat, open field–grown trees with broad canopies and curved leaders. Consequently, the style of vernacular timber framing that developed optimized the use of short, curved timbers.

Half-timber building in Ludlow, Shropshire.

The timbers were left exposed inside and out and infilled with wattle and daub or brick nogging. The timber pattern became the architecture—form followed function. This was called half-timber construction.

The oak timbers exposed to the elements weathered to a handsome silver-gray patina. During the Victorian period it became fashionable to paint the timbers black and the wattle and daub white. These painted half-timber buildings are now referred to as black and whites.

When my wife and I visited the English countryside, it was not hard to find examples of medieval timber frame homes. Many of them seemed to have changed little in 500 years, with the exception of modern windows and the occasional window air-conditioner. The home improvement craze that inspires American homeowners to continually alter their homes never caught on back in England.

Roof framed with crooked timbers—gatehouse at Lower Brockhampton, Herefordshire.

Timber Frame Homes of Weobley

The village of Weobley, in the Herefordshire area of England, is home to a delightful concentration of surviving medieval homes. It is not a museum, it is a living and breathing village that still looks much the same as it did 400 years ago.

Showing signs of structural distress.

Upper-floor jetty projects over sidewalk.

The black and white color scheme is optional.

Public art.

Cruck frame house.

Chapter One: European Ancestors | **Part One**

Thatched Roofs

Thatching was the roof of choice in the English countryside. Tile or slate was preferred in urban areas where the threat of fire was more menacing. Thatching was most commonly made of rye or wheat straw. Straw is the stalk of the plant left over after the grain had been threshed from it. The finest thatch was made from phragmites reed that grew in marshy areas.

Bundles of thatch were lashed to the roof frame and then shaped, shaved, and trimmed with a variety of specialty tools that would be unrecognizable to a roofer today. Thatched roofs proved to be durable, economical, and long lasting. They were well suited to the mild climate of Old England, but they did not fare as well in New England.

Thatching requires a very steep roof frame with a pitch greater than 12:12 (forty-five degrees). This explains why first-period homes in New England had such steep roofs.

Thatched country house.

Stone roof.

Phragmites reed made the best thatch.

Wattle and Daub

Walls were traditionally built of wattle and daube infill between the exposed timbers of the frame. The wattle was a lath of hazel saplings notched into the timbers and woven basket-style around riven oak slats called staves. Daub was a homemade plaster made of mud, straw, and—as a binder—the secret ingredient, cow dung, which gave the homes a special fragrance on damp days.

The daub was smeared over the wattle and smoothed by hand. For a more finished look, it could be covered with a lime plaster or sometimes just a limewash. The daub was applied to both sides of the wattle and became both the exterior and interior finish as well as the insulation.

Wattle and daub walls are easily eroded and required regular maintenance and recoating. It soon proved impractical in New England, where the climate was harsher than in Old England.

Wattle.

Daub.

Brick nogging.

Jetties

In crowded medieval towns and cities, houses were built right up to the edge of narrow streets. To gain extra living space, the upper floors were cantilevered over the street. These cantilevered projections are known as jetties. This practice dates back to the time of the Romans.

The jetties provided pedestrians some shelter from the elements and also from the slop buckets that were routinely emptied from the upper floor windows.

At some point it became fashionable to also build jetties on country homes. It was not done to gain additional living space, but to bring the look of urban sophistication to country homes.

Gatehouse, Stokesay Castle, Shropshire.

Upper-floor jetties on two sides.

Great Halls and Chimneys

In medieval manor homes, the whole family would gather in the great hall. It was a large space with a tall ceiling open to the rafters. The floor was earthen and in the center was a fire pit to take off the chill. Smoke from the fire would fill the space and exit through an open window or a hole in the roof. The space was dirty and smoke made your eyes sting, but the fire kept you warm.

Fireplaces with chimneys were not invented until the late sixteenth century. With the fire confined to a fireplace, the hall could be a much smaller, cozy space, since you no longer needed a high ceiling to hold the smoke. By the time the first Englishmen landed at Plymouth, fireplaces and chimneys were considered a modern convenience, and not all homes back in England had one.

Smoke-stained timbers of the Great Hall roof, Lower Brockhampton Manor, Herefordshire.

Tithe Barns

Most medieval farms did not have large barns. Hay was stored under an open roof called a rick. The climate was mild enough that farm animals could live outside year-round. During severe weather the animals were brought into the house to bed down with the rest of the family.

There were large, grand barns, but they were owned by the church and were called tithe barns. The tithe system existed in England from the time of the Norman conquest in 1066 until Henry VIII ascended to the throne in 1509 and wrestled political power away from the church. Everybody in a community was required to pay a tax to the church of ten percent of their annual agricultural production. The tax was called the tithe, which was Old English for a tenth. The church needed a place to store its booty of crops and sheep, so it built cathedral-like tithe barns.

Today, several restored tithe barns are open to the public and are well worth visiting. Sadly, many tourists miss out on this attraction. They waste their time doing silly things like watching the changing of the guard at Buckingham Palace. To say they are off the beaten path is an understatement. When you arrive, you are not entirely sure that you have, because there is minimal signage and no place to park except in the road. You must walk down a private drive, make a left turn down a garden path, and open a gate, and standing before you will be the tithe barn. You won't find anybody selling tickets or T-shirts. You need to unlatch the barn doors and let yourself in. By the door you will find a vending machine that will turn the lights on if you feed it a coin. You are then free to make yourself at home with no crowds to fight.

Leigh Court tithe barn, Worcestershire.

Foreign Influence

While the building traditions in New England originated primarily in Old England, England was not the only European power staking a claim in North America.

The Dutch established themselves in the Hudson River Valley and brought with them the Flemish building traditions of the lowlands. You will occasionally come upon a stray house of Dutch origin in western Connecticut or Massachusetts, but it is rare. The Dutch were close neighbors to New England and the Dutch and English influenced each other's building styles. The Dutch gave the English the sidewall shingle, the flared roof, and the split Dutch door, while the English gave the Dutch the gambrel roof.

The French had a presence in Northern New England, but they were mostly trappers and traders, not farmers, so they did not build permanent homes. There are many examples of old French architecture in Montreal and Quebec, but not much south of the Saint Lawrence River.

The Germans brought their own building traditions to Pennsylvania, but they were pretty much ignored by New Englanders.

The Swedes that settled in the Delaware River Valley brought a tradition of log house construction that the English had never seen. The innovation came too late to influence building in New England. Despite popular belief, log homes were not built in New England, but the New England Yankees did adopt log building when they moved west into the Mohawk Valley and Ohio Territory.

Log building was not a New England thing.

Trade Guilds

Trade guilds were a lot like unions today. If you wished to practice a building trade, you had to belong to the guild, and that meant that you needed connections. There were no trade schools, books on building construction, or how-to programs on TV. The only way to learn a building trade was to serve a seven-year apprenticeship under a master craftsman, after which you were given your own set of tools and sent on your way as a journeyman.

Everything was shrouded in secrecy to prevent outsiders from learning how to build without joining the guild. Guilds were empowered to pass ordinances to protect the "brotherhood and mystery" of the trade. A tradesman never performed a difficult task when somebody was watching. Nothing could be built without hiring guild carpenters and masons and paying the going rate. This guaranteed that guild tradesmen could make a good living.

Innovation was not encouraged. There was only one way of doing things—the guild way. Consequently, construction technology stagnated with very little change from century to century. If you wanted to try something different, or find a better way, then you had better take a slow boat to America where there was a building boom going on with a shortage of skilled tradesmen.

Chapter Two
FIRST PERIOD, 1620–1725

New England contained nothing "but a hideous and desolate wilderness, full of wild beasts and wild men."

—William Bradford, Plymouth Colony, 1620

Early First Period

The first permanent European settlement in New England was at Plymouth. These early settlers that we have come to know as the Pilgrims were, at the time, known as Separatists. They came to the New World to escape religious persecution in England after a decade of exile in Holland, where they did not fit in. At the time, they were considered religious extremists. Even the fundamentalist Puritans of Massachusetts Bay considered the Separatists to be the lunatic fringe of the Protestant faith. They came to the shores of New England to build a plantation where they could practice their faith without interference. They were not proponents of religious freedom; in fact they endeavored to practice their own breed of religious intolerance.

The Separatist came to the New World ill-equipped for survival. They arrived with few tools and little experience with farming, fishing, or building trades. The first winter they lived in hovels, tents made from sailcloth, and a few crude structures.

Those that survived the first winter set about the task of building more permanent shelter. The first homes were built in the medieval English tradition, but without the benefit of

One-room 1657 Alexander Knight house reproduction, Ipswitch, Massachusetts.

skilled tradesmen. They were small and cramped one-room homes with earthen floors.

The New England forest provided an ample supply of timber for building the frame. Timbers were roughly hewn with axes. There was no cellar or foundation. The timber posts were set in the ground like fence posts—a technique referred to as earth-fast construction.

The roofs were thatched with phragmite reed harvested from nearby marshes. Thatching soon proved ill-suited to the local climate. Exterior walls were constructed of wattle and daube, which also did not hold up well to the weather.

The fireplace and chimney were built of sticks and mud, which was not particularly fire resistant, but it was the best that they could do under the circumstances.

Little regard was given to architecture or style. Shelter from the elements was the overriding priority. As you might expect, the early homes did not survive long, but they served their purpose until proper homes could be built.

The Separatists of Plymouth were soon followed by English Puritan settlers who, in 1630, established the Massachusetts Bay colony in the Boston area. The Puritans were better organized and better equipped for survival. They brought with them tools, provisions, and skilled tradesmen. They also selected a better harbor with more fertile farmland than the Plymouth colony. Not surprisingly, the Massachusetts Bay colony expanded and prospered much more rapidly than the Separatists of the Plymouth colony.

The Puritans, led by John Winthrop, were Calvinists who believed that the Anglican Church of England was corrupt and too liberal. The Puritans had been tolerated in England and they were not escaping religious persecution. They came to America because they wished to live apart from the wretched Anglican sinners in England who threatened to pollute their faith. Puritans have acquired a reputation for not being a lot of fun. H. L. Mencken defined Puritanism as "the haunting fear that someone, somewhere, may be happy."

Hard times in England spurred a mass migration to the New World. Between 1630 and 1640, over 20,000 English men and women migrated to Massachusetts Bay. They soon outgrew Boston and began moving into the backcountry where they established new townships. New autonomous colonies were formed in Connecticut (1636), New Haven (1638), Rhode Island (1636), and New Hampshire (1641).

The Rhode Island colony was led by Roger Williams, a moderate Puritan banished from Boston for his tolerant beliefs. He preached the separation of church and state and believed that the Native Americans had rights, even if they were godless heathens. It is not hard to see why the Puritans viewed him as a dangerous character and referred to the colony as Rogue's Island. By contrast, the founders of Connecticut did not have any philosophical differences with the Boston Puritans; they were merely looking for better farmland.

First-Period Homes

The early New Englanders were typical of medieval England. They were devoutly Christian but also superstitious—they really believed in pagan omens and things like witches. Few were literate, and those who were only read from one book. They were hard-working and industrious. It wasn't long before their farms were prospering and they could build proper homes for themselves.

When thatched roofs proved impractical, wood shingles became the only way to roof a house. At first roof shingles were made of hand-split or riven red oak and later pine, but they did not prove durable. Eventually, decay-resistant white cedar became the preferred wood

Parson Capen house, circa 1683, Topsfield, Massachusetts.

John Ward house, circa 1684, Salem, Massachusetts.

species for roof shingles where it was available.

First-period roofs were very steep because that was the tradition in England and a necessity for a thatched roof. It took nearly a century for housewrights to come to the realization that roofs could be built with a much shallower pitch if they were roofed with wood shingles.

When wattle and daub exterior walls proved to be as impractical as thatched roofs, walls were covered with riven oak clapboards, but wattle and daub still served as the interior wall finish and insulation. When lime for plaster became readily available in the early eighteenth

Decorative drops were actually the bottom of the second-floor timber posts. Stanley Whitman house, circa 1720, Farmington, Connecticut.

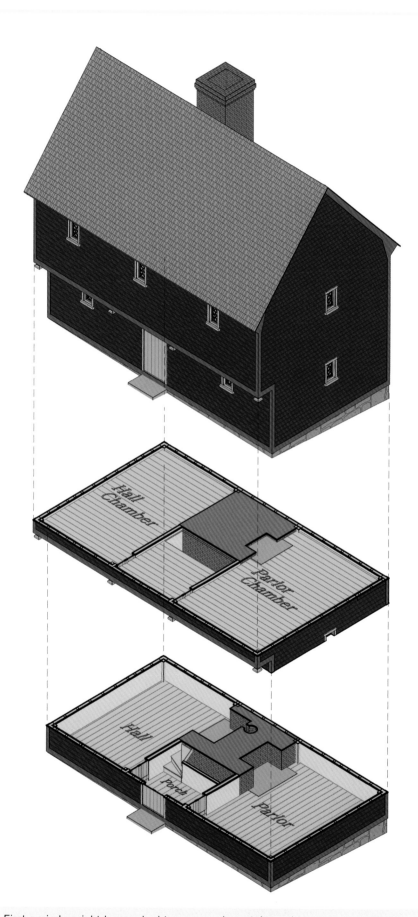

century, plaster replaced wattle and daub as the interior wall finish.

The timber framing was exposed on the ceilings. The timbers were chamfered and planed smooth since they were being shown off. It wasn't that builders liked the look of a beamed ceiling, they just didn't have lime to make plaster.

Glass was expensive and hard to come by. Consequently, windows were few and small. Operable windows were casements with small, diamond-shaped glass panes called quarrels, joined with lead cames.

Chimneys were positioned in the center of the house to maximize the heat radiated into the space during the long New England winters. The kitchen fireplace was large enough to walk into and chimney flues were large enough for a chimney sweep to climb. Built of brick bonded with clay mortar, their proportions were massive.

In the Old World tradition, many homes had projecting jetties with carved post finials called drops. The rational for building jetties had long since been forgotten, but the tradition lingered. Some architectural historians have postulated that they were for defense against hostile Indians, but that is just plain silly.

The finest homes of the day were two stories with two rooms on each floor—a hall and parlor on the first floor separated by a narrow entrance foyer called a porch with a winding stair. They were called upright houses.

First-period upright houses had two rooms downstairs and two rooms upstairs.

Parlor of the Appleton-Taylor-Mansfield house, circa 1680, Saugus, Massachusetts, restored by Wallace Nutting.

To describe the living conditions in first-period homes as austere is being kind. Rooms were small and crowded, with low ceilings. Natural light was scarce and rooms were gloomy, even on a sunny day. Interior designers today refer to first-period colonial architecture as primitive and that is an accurate description.

Only a small handful of these homes have survived intact and most of them are museum homes. By the second quarter of the eighteenth century, they were considered unsuitable for habitation by respectable families and were converted into barns, woodsheds, or kitchen ells. Those that have survived as homes have been so extensively altered as to be unrecognizable.

When everyone was weather-minded, no one would have dreamed of building a house without the entrance being to the south and the greatest roof slant to the north. . . New England architecture was designed by New England weather.

—Eric Sloane

Lovingly restored, circa 1759 saltbox in Morris, Connecticut. The rear roofline breaks where the lean-to was added. Note that the foundation has settled on the right side of the photo, but the siding and windows have been leveled.

The saltbox, with its awkward asymmetrical roof, is a uniquely New England building form. It is ideally suited to the harsh climate, with south-facing windows to catch the sun and a long roof fending off the brutal north winds.

At the time, the notion of orienting a home to face the road was absurd. Most houses and barns were built to face the sun.

A saltbox was for storing salt.

The first saltbox appeared in the mid-seventeenth century. The idea did not come from some popular architect of the day, it just happened. Nobody knows who built the first saltbox. It started innocently enough; somebody got the idea of building a kitchen with a lean-to roof on the back of his crowded house. He was probably tired of his wife complaining about having to cook dinner in the keeping room fireplace with the rest of the family crowded into the room. It was such an easy way to add on, with no alterations needed to the roof or building structure, and it functioned so well that his neighbors started converting their two-story homes to saltboxes. Before you know it, the idea had spread throughout New England. By the end of the seventeenth century, people were building their new homes as saltboxes.

A saltbox was a household item found in every kitchen for storing salt. Salt was a valuable commodity used for preserving meats, not just for seasoning. The saltbox was usually found hanging on the wall next to the fireplace, where the heat would keep the salt dry. It had a sloping, hinged lid

Room Nomenclature

Rooms went by different names than the ones we use today, so we have to get the terminology down.

The hall was not a hallway. It was actually the most important room in the house. The name was a carryover from the great halls of medieval manor homes. It was the place where the whole family hung out. Before there was a separate kitchen, the hall was where meals were prepared and taken.

In later homes, where the hall had its own door to the outside, it was called a keeping room. When a family member passed away, services were held at home. Since the keeping room had a direct door to the outside, it was the only room that the coffin could get into, so that is where the body was "kept." A wake was held to give the dearly departed an opportunity to wake up in

the event that their passing had been misdiagnosed.

The parlor was the best room of the house, where guests would be entertained and your finest possessions displayed. It also doubled as the master bedroom and was often the only room with an "off the floor" bed.

The front entrance foyer and stair hall was called a porch. This terminology has misled many historians to believe that an older house once had a covered porch on the exterior. The porch was later referred to as the passage.

The rooms on the second floor were called chambers and were named after the room they were above. So there was the hall chamber and the parlor chamber. They weren't called bedrooms because people actually slept in every room of the house.

The kitchen was exactly what you would expect. Adjacent to the kitchen was a small room for food storage called a buttery or a pantry. There was often another small room adjacent to the kitchen that was called a bedroom. It was little bigger than a closet and the bed filled the room. It was reserved for guests and situations where privacy was needed. Some people refer to it today as the borning room, but that was not a term used at the time. The notion that the room would only be used for childbirth is a bit ridiculous. If you had to give it another name, conception room would be more accurate.

The attic was called the garret. It wasn't a space for just storing stuff that you didn't want to throw away, it was used as unfinished living space—often for servants or children.

The Ogden house, circa 1750, Fairfield, Connecticut.

Ethan Allen homestead, circa 1787, Burlington, Vermont.

that some thought resembled the roofline of their home. Personally I never saw much resemblance, but then again, when I gaze at the stars in the night sky I do not see dragons, bears, or chariots, either.

Saltbox roofs were not exclusive to New England. A few were built in the southern colonies as well, but southerners called them cat slide roofs.

The one-and-a-half-story cape was built everywhere in New England, not just on Cape Cod. It was a practical and economical home to build, although a bit cramped. As farms grew and became prosperous, cape houses were enlarged and expanded everywhere, except on Cape Cod where prosperity was more elusive. Consequently, Cape Cod has the largest collection of surviving capes.

Cape houses are still affordable to build. Following World War II, when William Levitt was mass-producing affordable suburban homes, he built capes.

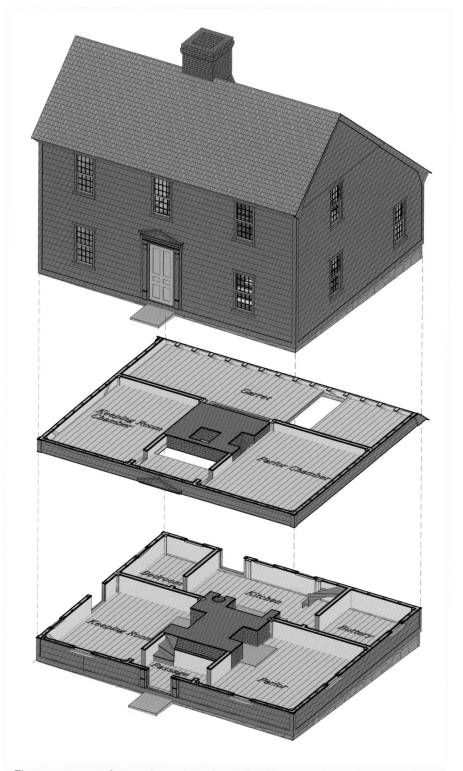

The arrangement of rooms in a saltbox is predicable.

We are more thoroughly an enlightened people
. . . than perhaps any under heaven.

—Benjamin Franklin

Sloan-Raymond-Fitch house, circa 1772, Wilton, Connecticut.

The Georgian Period officially began in 1714 when the first of four Georges ascended to the throne in England. In New England it was the age of reason—the enlightenment. Medieval thinking had been replaced by science and an intellectual quest for knowledge. New Englanders no longer considered themselves Puritans—they were Yankees. Farms prospered and New Englanders were living a better life than their counterparts in England. A spirit of self-determination would eventually strain ties with Mother England to the breaking point.

Restored Stratton Tavern, circa 1763, now in Concord, Massachusetts, was moved from Northfield, Massachusetts. Courtesy of Early New England Restoration.

When people think of Georgian architecture, they envision stately brick buildings, not realizing that the brick is optional. Georgian homes were elegant, particularly compared to the primitive first-period homes of the prior century—they don't give the feeling of roughing it.

Georgian architecture emulated the work of the Italian Renaissance architect Andrea Palladio (1508–1580). Homes had formal details and were perfectly symmetrical, with the entrance door smack in the center. Windows were arranged in a regular pattern around the entranceway.

Inside, wall and ceiling surfaces were plastered or covered with raised panel wainscoting. The rough timber frame was no longer suitable for viewing and was concealed behind the plaster or cased with finished woodwork.

The center chimney floor plan remained popular, but by the second half of the eighteenth century was slowly being replaced by the center hall plan with two symmetrical chimneys and rooms flanking a gracious stair hall. The kitchen and work spaces were moved into an ell behind the house.

Some architectural elements that are prolific in colonial revival homes were conspicuously absent from Georgian homes—exterior shutters, dormers, and mantel shelves over the fireplace. They would all arrive on the scene soon enough as the federal period dawned.

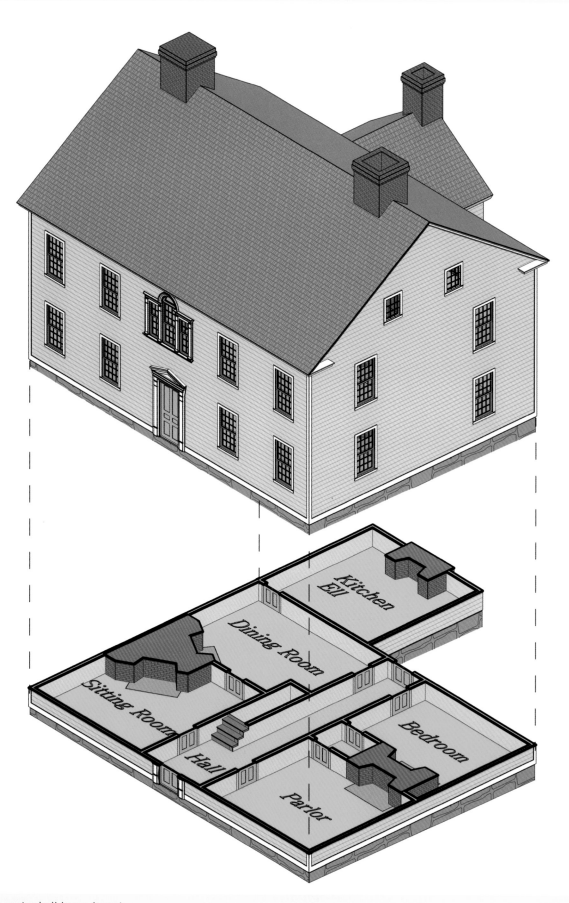

Spacious center-hall home layout.

Chapter Five
FEDERAL PERIOD, 1790–1820

Federal home in Westport, Connecticut.

With the signing of the Treaty of Paris in 1783, the American Revolution ended. The colonial period came to a close and the federal period was born. Americans became instilled with a euphoric sense of optimism and nationalism. They yearned for a new architectural style for their new republic. For inspiration they naturally turned to Mother England, where the latest rage was Adamesque architecture. Americans would no longer be ruled by England, but that did not stop them from emulating her.

Robert Adam and his brother James were Scottish-born architects and interior designers who had become architectural rock stars in London. Robert had studied in Italy, and

Salem Towne house, circa 1796, Old Sturbridge Village, moved from Charlton, Massachusetts.

upon returning home went into partnership with his brother James. They developed the Adam style inspired by classical Roman architecture. Books of their works were published and they were widely imitated.

Federal architecture maintained a lot of the features of the Georgian period. The exterior façade became less formal and the detailing more delicate. Symmetry was now optional and some homes had their entrance door off to one side. Roof slopes became shallow and hip roofs were popular. Cornices became more prominent with broad frieze boards, sometimes ornamented with Roman urn and garland motifs. Corner boards became wider, often embellished with

Federal-period parlor. *Courtesy of Historic Deerfield.*

fluting. Shutters, painted contrasting colors, flanked the windows.

Entrances became more inviting. Transom and side-light windows framed the door, bringing natural light into the stair hall. Porch roofs were built over the entrance to protect visitors from the elements—an idea that is so practical it is a wonder that nobody thought of it before.

Inside, rooms were more spacious with larger windows and taller ceilings. Fireplace surrounds became focal points and mantel shelfs over the fireplace were introduced, offering a place to display one's finest possessions. The center chimney was nearing extinction. The stair was now a grand affair with turned balusters and newels, graciously inviting one to the second-floor bedrooms, which now had closets.

Hadwen house, circa 1845, Nantucket, Massachusetts, with a grand Ionic columned portico.

By 1820 the American Revolution was a distant memory. The last of the founding fathers, Thomas Jefferson and John Adams, passed away in 1826, fifty years to the day after the signing of the Declaration of Independence. The once shaky, fledgling federal government was now established, although with bickering in Congress it was no less dysfunctional than it is today. The idea of a democratic republic had been regarded as a bold experiment a few decades earlier, but it was now clear that the United States was here to stay.

Washington DC had been rebuilt after being burned by the British in the War of 1812. The war had turned into a debacle for the Americans. But with the conclusion of the war, there was no longer a credible threat of America being taken over by a European power. Even Napoleon had given up his ambitions to conquer America and had sold France's holdings with the Louisiana Purchase in 1803.

Western expansion was in full swing and Americans embraced the Monroe Doctrine. America was destined to be an

Humble Greek revival farmhouse, Washington, Connecticut.

empire. But no one was abandoning their farm in New England to go west. Life was too good at home. Farms were prospering. The forested wilderness had long since been cleared and tamed. New Englanders were living the dream.

In 1821, Greece was fighting its own war of independence from the Turks. Back in New England there was a feeling of kinship with the Greeks and their struggle. Ancient Greece was the first democracy and a role model for the young American republic. These warm feelings for Greece inspired the Greek revival movement.

Classical architecture had long been considered the only proper style for important public buildings. In the 1820s, it became fashionable to also build your home to resemble an ancient Greek temple. The most conspicuous and ostentatious examples had grand porticos lined with Ionic or Doric columns, but even humble farmhouses adopted elements borrowed from the Greeks.

Houses were rotated ninety degrees so that their gable ends, now sporting pediments, faced the front. It became popular to paint your house white to resemble marble. If you could not afford a grand portico, you could at least adorn the façade with a few fluted pilasters. The Greek mania was so big, it is a wonder that New Englanders were not throwing toga parties.

Chapter Seven
COLONIAL REVIVAL, 1890–PRESENT

Until one day the country looked more like it
used to than it ever had before.

—Garrison Keillor

Twentieth-century garrison colonial.

The industrial revolution ushered in a new way of building houses with factory-made components that could be shipped by rail and assembled on site. With this new building technology came a new style of architecture—Victorian, with gingerbread trim and decoration. But by the 1890s, many had become weary of self-indulgent Victorian architecture and yearned for homes reminiscent of an earlier, simpler time. The colonial revival was born as a backlash to Victorian architecture. By the 1920s, the colonial revival movement had hit full stride and Victorian homes were history.

The colonial revival style is still alive today. Since the 1920s, modern architecture has come and gone and come again, but colonial homes have never stopped being popular.

What passes for a colonial home today has only the vaguest resemblance to an eighteenth-century antique home. It has a pitched roof, double-hung windows with shutters, and horizontal siding, but that is where the similarity ends.

This reconstruction of a colonial revival house in Westport, Connecticut, is easily mistaken for a 200-year-old home.

Wallace Nutting (1861–1941), Champion of the Colonial Revival

Wallace Nutting did more to promote the colonial revival movement than any one hundred men of his day. A recovering Congregational minister turned entrepreneur, he turned nostalgia and quaintness into big business.

As a minister in Providence, Rhode Island, his duties included counseling members of his congregation on their personal problems. This proved to be too heavy a burden and eventually led to an emotional breakdown. Citing health issues, Nutting left the ministry in 1904 to pursue his true passion.

Nutting yearned for a return to the morality and values of colonial times—to a time and place he called Old America. He believed that America, in his day, had become morally corrupt. It was a time of industrialization, cities overcrowded with immigrants, a bloody and pointless World War, and the Roaring Twenties, followed by a crippling economic depression.

He built an empire of inter-related business ventures, each of which promoted the others, and all of them based on the fantasy world of Old America. His first venture was mass-marketing affordable art to middle-class consumers. He produced a collection of hand-tinted photographs depicting pastoral landscapes and Old American images that he called colonials. His colonials were set in a room that had a fireplace and was furnished with early American furniture and oval braided rugs. They always featured a young woman, dressed in a gown, shawl, and bonnet, sipping tea or performing some domestic task, such as baking a pie or spinning yarn. He portrayed women in their proper role as he perceived it. He deplored the attitude of modern wom-

Hand-tinted colonial photograph *An Afternoon Tea.*

en, particularly those pushy suffragettes and scandalous flappers. He employed a brood of young women who painted the color on the photographs and also posed for them.

Nutting collected early American furniture and was particularly fond of furniture from the seventeenth century, which he called the Pilgrim century. He manufactured reproductions of his furniture collection so that you could furnish your own home with replicas of the pieces depicted in his photographs. He also manufactured reproduction iron hardware and braided rugs. Braided rugs did not actually exist in colonial times, but Nutting believed that they should have.

Eventually, Nutting sold his furniture collection to J. P. Morgan in 1924. Morgan donated it to the Wadsworth Atheneum in Hartford, where the collection is still on exhibit.

Nutting purchased a chain of historic homes in Massachusetts, Con-

Wallace Nutting.

necticut, and New Hampshire. He restored the homes and opened them to the public as house museums. He was not hung up on historic accuracy—he restored them to what he thought they should have looked like. The houses were furnished with his furniture collection and braided rugs. He photographed his colonials in the houses and proudly displayed his collection of hand-tinted photographs on the walls.

A prolific author, Nutting formed his own publishing company, Old America Company, to produce his books. He wrote books on early American furniture, clocks, and iron hardware. It wasn't long before Nutting was regarded as the leading authority on colonial-period furniture and decorative arts.

He wrote a popular series of travellogs, each featuring a particular state. He titled the books *Massachusetts Beautiful*, *Connecticut Beautiful*, *Vermont Beautiful*, and so on—you get the idea. The books were filled with his landscape and colonial photographs. It was a time when automobile touring was becoming popular. Armed with his books, you could leave the city and roam the New England countryside, visiting his chain of house museums and other Old America sites.

There was something about Wallace Nutting's idea of Old America that struck a note with people and launched the colonial revival.

The Ironmaster's House in Saugus, Massachusetts, was Nutting's first museum house.

Chapter Eight
SEAPORT TOWNHOUSES

While New England farms were doing well, the truly wealthy were the merchants and ship owners living in the seaport towns of Newport, Salem, and Portsmouth. Many were making fortunes in merchant shipping, smuggling, and privateering. Naturally they built stylish homes for themselves.

Newport, Rhode Island, was the most active seaport in colonial America. Visitors to Newport today rush off to see the Breakers and other mansions of the rich and famous. They miss out on the town's real architectural treasures—the fine Georgian townhouses hidden on the side streets surrounding the downtown waterfront.

Crowninshield-Bentley house, circa 1727, Salem, Massachusetts.

Georgian townhouse, Newport, Rhode Island.

Nantucket

On the island of Nantucket, fortunes were being made in whale oil. The frugal Quaker ship owners built fine homes for themselves that were nice but simple. The fashionable, high-style detailing popular in the mainland seaports was considered too garish for Nantucket.

While largely similar to Georgian and federal homes on the mainland, Nantucket homes had some unique features. The exterior siding was almost always weathered, silver-gray shingles. They often had rooftop decks that have acquired the name widow's watch. The name is a romantic fantasy. Despite the popular myth, a widow's watch was not used by ship captains' wives searching the horizon for their loved one's return. Whalers went to sea for years at a time—their wives had better things to do with their time while they were away. A widow's watch does serve as a breezy outdoor living space with a great view of the harbor.

The thing that makes Nantucket architecture special is the way the homes on the island, both antique and new, complement each other. The entire island has been designated a historic district. Every new home or remodeling project must be approved by the Historic District Commission, which has strict guidelines for architectural style and details. It is a bureaucratic hassle for architects and builders, but it has been a huge success for the community.

One of Nantucket's many gray ladies.

Chapter Eight: Seaport Townhouses | **Part One**

I like a man who likes to see a fine barn as
well as a good tragedy.

—Ralph Waldo Emerson

Every rural antique home, at one time, had a barn out back, along with a variety of other farm buildings. Typically the barn would be built before the house since it was more important to the success of the farm.

When farming life became a thing of the past in New England, many barns fell into disrepair. Most of the surviving barns are little more than rotted hulks, just waiting for a winter snowfall to bring them crashing down.

Winter's bitter harvest—another once proud, neglected barn bites the dust under the weight of snow.

English Barns

Early New England barns were called English barns. They did not actually resemble barns in Old England, but were distinctively different from the Dutch barns of the Hudson River Valley and the German barns of Pennsylvania.

English barns were timber frame structures three bays wide. Symmetry was optional and the bays were usually of unequal width.

The center bay was called the threshing bay, since that is where crops would be threshed to separate the grain from the plant. The crops were given a "thrashing" by beating them with a tool called a flail that resembled ninja nunchucks. The floor boards of the threshing bay were tightly fitted planks to prevent the grain from falling through the joints. A board called a threshold was placed across the doorway during threshing to keep the grain in.

The barn doors were on the side wall and opened into the threshing bay. When there was no threshing going on, the threshing bay would be used to park the wagon or carriage. The side bays were used as animal pens and for grain storage. The loft space above was the hay mow (pronounced like cow) for storing winter fodder.

Barns that were built into a hillside were called bank barns. They had a lower level that could be accessed from the back like a walk-out basement. The lower level was usually reserved for the hogs. Manure would be shoveled through trap doors in the floor to feed the hogs below.

English barn, Old Sturbridge Village.

Yankee Barns

Freeman barn, Old Sturbridge Village, moved from Charlton, Massachusetts.

As farms grew in the nineteenth century, the English barns became too small and obsolete. Farmers built new, larger barns called Yankee barns or New England barns.

The Yankee barn was rotated ninety degrees from an English barn and the barn doors were on the end wall. Having the doors on the end wall was an advantage in inclement weather—you no longer got drenched coming in and out of the door from water pouring off the eaves.

If the site was level, doors would be put at both ends of the barn so a wagon, hitched to a team of horses, could drive through instead of backing in. Putting a team of horses in reverse could be an exasperating experience.

Yankee barns often had siding, windows, and trim that matched the main house. Robert Frost Farm, Derry, New Hampshire.

Connected Barns

A Maine barn connected to the house.

In the nineteenth century, it became fashionable to connect the barn to the house in Southern Maine and New Hampshire. The barn did not connect directly to the house, there was usually a train of buildings—the house, ell, woodshed, and a workshop, with the barn as the caboose.

Connecting the barn to the house was actually a foolish and reckless thing to do. Barns frequently caught fire, so keeping it away from the house only made sense. Also, when the barn housed animals, it acquired a very distinctive fragrance that improved with distance.

New England farms in the nineteenth century practiced mixed agriculture. They grew a variety of crops as well as raising cows, sheep, hogs, and chickens. They also practiced home industry to make ends meet. Every farmer had a trade—as a cooper, potter, farrier, or cobbler. By connecting the farm buildings, the mixed agriculture and home industry operations could be more efficient.

New Uses for Old Barns and Old Uses for New Barns

In the eighteenth century, it was commonplace to repurpose an old house into a barn. Today it is more common to convert an old barn into a house. Timber barn frames are actually very easy to dismantle and move. It is much easier to repair the timbers after the frame has been dismantled rather than trying to perform the repairs in place. It is rare to find an old barn that does not need quite a bit of repair work, and even rarer to find one sitting on a decent foundation. So if you come across an old barn that is down on its luck, it is an act of kindness to adopt it and bring it home with you.

While many people truly enjoy barn living, I have always believed that a barn sitting by itself looks kind of lonely. A barn looks best when it has an antique home to keep it company.

I have found having a barn next to my antique house to be indispensable. I frankly don't understand how some people live without a barn and I know that I would not want to. Rather than adopt an old barn, I built a new timber frame barn near my house that I use as a workshop and to park my tractors. It is my man cave.

A barn is also a good place for a kid's recreation room, in-law apartment, or other objectionable uses that you don't want in your home.

A barn connected to the back of your antique house is a good place for a garage. You can disguise it as a Maine-style connected barn and it will blend right in.

My new old barn.

My dream workshop upstairs.

A home for my tractors downstairs.

Chapter Ten
DATING TIPS

Have you ever noticed those plaques on the front of antique homes, proudly displaying a date, and wondered how they know the house's birthday? Sometimes it is based on rigorous research and other times just plain wishful thinking.

It seems as though every antique homeowner wants their home to have a pedigree. It is prestigious to have the oldest surviving home in the community. But if it is not the oldest, the next best thing is to predate the American Revolution. I have observed that there are a disproportionate number of antique homes displaying the date 1773. I don't believe there were actually enough housewrights alive in 1773 to have built all of the homes claiming to have been built that year.

Don't believe everything you read on a sign.

Documentary Evidence

Researching land records can give clues to the age of a home. Land deeds tell the story of when the property changed hands and who owned it. Probate records tell you what they owned when they died. If they had a house, it will likely be mentioned in their will.

From the land records it is possible to determine the approximate date that a house was first built on a site. But the antique home standing today may not be the same house that was first built on the property. The original house may have burnt down or been converted to a woodshed that has long since fallen in on itself. Your home may have been built much later.

Physical Evidence

Let your antique house speak to you; it will tell you its story if you know how to listen. There are clues to its age hiding in plain sight.

Examine the saw marks on timbers and the underside of floorboards. Were they pit sawn, water mill sawn, or circular sawn?

Examine the timber joinery. Was it square rule layout or scribe rule?

Examine the nails used to hold down the attic floor boards. Are they hand-forged or cut nails?

Examine the door hardware. What type of hinges and latches were used?

Each of these building elements will be discussed in greater detail later, so keep reading.

The Fairbanks house, Dedham, Massachusetts, is believed to be the oldest surviving timber frame house in North America. The chimney proudly displays the date 1636. Recent dendro dating studies suggest that 1641 is more accurate.

Stylistic Clues

The architectural style of a home will give a clue of its age. Is it Georgian, federal, or Greek revival? The latest architectural fashions of Europe were first adopted in coastal seaport towns. It sometimes took a couple of decades more before they were adopted in the remote rural communities of northern New Hampshire or western Massachusetts.

Keep in mind that the stylistic elements may be from a later remodeling. Your house could be older than its style suggests.

Dendrochronology

Dendrochronology is the study of tree rings. If you examine the end grain of any piece of wood, the tree rings are evident. Each ring represents one year in the life of the tree that the timber was milled from. The climate at the time a tree grew is recorded in its rings.

A bore sample prepared for examination.

A bore sample.

History revealed in tree rings.

In dry years, the tree grew slowly and the rings are narrow, and in wet years they are wide.

Dendrochronologists have studied and recorded the growth pattern of New England trees that date to before the Separatists landed at Plymouth. There are now dendrochronology databases for particular regions of New England and particular species of trees.

To date an antique home, approximately a dozen pencil-size samples are taken from various timbers in the frame using a core drill called an increment borer. The patterns of tree rings in the samples are compared, under a microscope, to the database for the region where the house is located. The precise year that the trees were felled can be determined.

Trees were typically felled shortly before being milled and incorporated into a frame. It is reasonable to conclude that the construction start date is within a year of when the timbers were cut.

I have had clients get angry when they got the report from the dendrochronologist because in their hearts they just knew that their house was older than the report concluded. But the facts are the facts. If you don't want to know the truth, don't ask the question.

Bill Flynt extracts a sample from a floor joist with an increment borer.

You must learn from the mistakes of others. You can't possibly live long enough to make them all yourself.
—Sam Levenson

Restoring and renovating an antique home is often an experience of a life-time—sometimes even a labor of love. If things are well planned, it can be a real thrill—the most fun you ever had with your clothes on. But if you rush in without thinking things through, it can quickly turn into a nightmarish project from hell. It can bring your family together or tear it apart.

Chapter Eleven
GETTING STARTED

An antique home restoration project is a major undertaking that will consume copious amounts of monetary and emotional capital. Don't just rush in to it. Thorough planning and realistic expectations are crucial to the project's success.

Assessing the Condition

Before you start, figure out what you have—what is old, what is new, what is real, and what is fake. You also need to figure out what condition everything is in—what needs repair and what is beyond repair.

When you bought your house, you probably got a home inspection. Banks usually won't give a loan without one. Home inspection reports are usually of limited value in planning a restoration project. Home inspectors typically have limited experience with antique homes. They get most of their business from real estate agent referrals. If they write a report that is too thorough, or sounds too negative, they will be labeled a deal killer and referrals will dry up.

When I bought my antique house in 1981, I went in with the expectation that I would need to completely replace the electrical, plumbing, heating, roofing, kitchen, and bathrooms. I assumed that the house was uninsulated and that I would probably find rotted wood that needed replacement everywhere I looked. I also assumed that I would have to deal with lead-based paint, asbestos pipe insulation, and an aging underground oil tank. With those expectations, there was not much that the home inspector could tell me that made any difference.

If the house was livable when you bought it, live in it awhile and get to know it. Take off the rose-colored glasses that you

Start with a thorough engineering evaluation of the structure.

wore when you first saw the house and look carefully at every floorboard and window sash. Let the house talk to you.

Assemble your team before you begin. Pick an architect and builder who are experienced with antique homes and also share your vision. They should each inspect your house from top to bottom, and they will each have different observations. Your architect should measure the house and prepare drawings of the existing conditions. Now you are ready to start planning.

Budget Realities

Be honest about what you can afford. Any home-building project can suck up money at a frightening rate and restoration projects do it more viciously than new construction. The one thing you can count on is that the project will cost a lot more than you thought it would. There will be unforeseen conditions uncovered during construction that will be expensive to deal with. Expect the unexpected. Once you have a realistic budget for the project, double it.

If what I said about construction costs scares you, good—you need to be scared.

To Gut or Not to Gut

The most critical strategic decision you must make is whether to gut the plaster walls and ceilings or leave the plaster in place. Removing plaster and lath is a dirty, dusty job, but if you bite the bullet and get the plaster out of the way at the start of the project, everything after that will go smoother. Electrical, plumbing, ductwork, and insulation are much easier to install with the plaster out of the way. Gutting the plaster also exposes the structure so that all the structural problems can be identified and rectified.

The disadvantage to removing the plaster is that you lose the plaster that might be in perfectly serviceable condition. If you replace the plaster with drywall, the look and feel is just not the same.

Stripping away the plaster skin to reveal the guts of the house.

Before you make a decision, assess the plaster condition. If it is cracked, crumbling, and the keys to the lath are broken, the decision is easy—nuke it. If it is in good condition, you might want to save it. In early homes the plaster was installed after the woodwork, and the plaster can be removed without disturbing wainscoting or door and window trim. In later homes, the trim was installed after the plaster, so you can't remove the plaster without removing all of the trim as well. Make a few probes through the plaster around the doors and windows to determine how it was done before you decide to gut.

For my own house, I chose to leave the plaster in place in the original 1809 portion of the house, with the exception of the living room ceiling that was badly damaged from a plumbing leak. In the 1890 and 1930 additions, I gutted the plaster and lath. I just had a gut feeling about it.

Living Through It

The next major decision involves whether to live in the house while it is being restored. This is usually an easy one. My advice is don't even think about it. Rent an apartment, move in with your in-laws, park a motor home in the driveway—do anything except try to live in the house.

If you have a builder doing the work, you will just be in everybody's way and the project will cost a lot more to complete. Not to mention, living with plaster dust on everything you own is not just unpleasant, it is downright unhealthy.

When I restored my own house, I did live in it. I was young and single and used to roughing it. It was a lot like camping without having to leave home. I was also doing most of the work myself, so I wasn't in anybody else's way. I would not have tried it with a family.

So if you don't want your spouse and kids to leave you, find someplace else for you and your loved ones to live while your house is being worked on.

Salvaging and Scavenging

I am forever scrounging architectural salvage yards and flea markets for old house parts I can repurpose. I don't usually go looking for anything in particular, but when I see something that catches my attention, I grab it and give it a new home.

In my professional life, I occasionally stumble upon architectural treasures destined for the dumpster. I sometimes have clients who are converting an antique house into professional offices or retail space and have no interest in trying to save the old doors, fireplace mantels, window sash, or floor boards. In those instances I back up my truck and fill it up.

Spare parts have always come in handy in restoring my antique home, and especially when I was building my reinterpreted antique home. As long as the spare

Fireplace mantel salvaged from a fire-damaged home.

parts are of the right period and style, they fit right in and nobody can tell they are not original.

Conjecturing

In restoring an antique house, you will invariably encounter situations where architectural elements were disfigured or removed during previous renovations. You want to restore the house to the way it looked originally, but there are no records of what it looked like. Then it is time to do some good old-fashioned conjecturing and come up with a concept of what it might have looked like.

Conjectural Restoration—The Porch

The sunroom under the north wing had to go.

The final product.

My home has a second-floor addition on the north side with an open porch below. The addition was built circa 1890. In 1930 the porch was enclosed to create a sunroom. When I purchased the house in 1981, the sunroom was in pretty bad shape. The timber sills and post bases were rotted and the second floor had dropped more than two inches. I proceeded to tear out the sunroom and jack up the second floor to level it. I then replaced the foundations and post bases. I decided to open the porch up as it originally was. Problem was, there was no record of what it originally looked like—time for some conjecturing.

The first step in a conjectural design is to search for a historical precedent in a similar period home. It did not take long for me to find a home about the same age and style in nearby New Canaan, Connecticut. It had graceful arches between the porch columns. It was the perfect design solution.

I also looked to my own house for inspiration. One of the architectural motifs that repeats over and over, both inside and outside, is the elliptical archway. So it was a natural solution to make the porch arches elliptical rather than circular. The final solution turned out looking perfectly appropriate, even if it may not be historically accurate.

The inspiration.

Hand Tools vs. Power Tools

When my antique house was built, there was no such thing as a table saw, and if there had been, there would have been no place to plug it in. But if the housewrights that built my house were able to use power tools, I have no doubt that they would have jumped at the chance. They used the most efficient tools available and had no aversion to utilizing technology to make their job easier.

The advantage of power tools is that you accomplish more in less time than with hand tools. But more importantly, you can get the job done with less skill. You don't need a seven-year apprenticeship to be able to rip a board to a straight line.

If you are a purist and want the finished work to look like it was crafted by the old masters with authentic tool marks, hand tools are the only way to go. I have found that the best hand tools, with a few exceptions, are antique tools. The old tools tend to hold a sharp edge better than modern tools. I make a habit of roaming flea markets for old tools that have fallen on hard times.

As my skills improve, I find myself gravitating more and more to using hand tools. It is a much more pleasant and calming experience—a little zen-like. Working with power tools is a noisy experience with sawdust blowing in your face. Working with sharp hand tools is quiet, and you are making wood shavings instead of dust.

I am not ready to give up my power tools just yet, but there is a place for both power and hand tools in my shop.

Hand planing a board.

Jacking and Leveling

Few antique homes are plumb, level, and square. Most have rocking and rolling floors with out-of-square door frames. Real estate agents call it charming. I call it structural distress. These undulations and deformations that we have come to expect in antique homes are sometimes caused by foundation settlement, but more often are caused by structural deficiencies, or structural deterioration such as rotted sills.

A few years ago, when my wife and I visited England, we were on a tour of a medieval manor house when she happened to notice signs of obvious structural distress in a badly sagging timber frame. She was educated as an artist and has no formal engineering training, but she has been hanging around me long enough to be able spot and diagnose structural issues fairly accurately. She happened to mention to the docent that the timber sills were clearly rotted and they really should do something about that. The docent's response was priceless—"Oh no. It is perfectly alright. It is supposed to be like that. It is a very old building and it will be around long after we are gone."

I hear this kind of ridiculous stuff all the time from builders and people in the trades. If you have an expert try to tell you that your house is just settling and it is supposed to do that, find yourself another expert who knows what he is talking about.

Before you can fix a sagging structure, you first must figure out what is making it sag. Sometimes it is obvious—a rotted corner post or a missing column in the cellar. Other times you might need an engineer. Once the cause has been identified, it is usually a simple matter to find the cure.

You might choose to live with the rocking and rolling after the structural issue that caused it has been corrected. Maybe it is charming, but if the deformations are excessive and you get seasick walking across the living room, you might find it more spooky than charming.

You can reverse some of the structural deformations by jacking, but you will never be able to get everything dead level. The structural timbers that have deflected over the centuries have gotten used to the deformation and will not give it up without a fight. Jacking should be done very slowly over the course of weeks to give the structure a chance to acclimate to being leveled.

As you jack the structure to level it, plaster walls will crack. Doors that closed before will stick and bind. Plan on shaving doors and window sashes when you are done. Aggressive jacking can also fracture timber joints, so take it slow. The house will talk to you as you jack it up. You will hear snaps, crackles, and pops. If you hear a loud bang, than you went too far and busted something and it is time to call the engineer back.

Hiring Professionals and Contractors

Unless you have the skills to design and build the project entirely yourself, you are going to need some professional help. You will need an architect to design the project and prepare drawings. You will also need a builder and a variety of specialty subcontractors such as carpenters, plasterers, electricians, and plumbers.

There is a popular notion that when selecting a contractor you should get at least three bids and award the project to the lowest bidder. If you follow that course, no good can come of it. If you are lucky, the project will be completed with barely adequate workmanship. If you are not so lucky, you will have a project from hell with skyrocketing extra charges, substandard workmanship, disappearing tradesmen, and a big bill from your attorney to clean up the mess.

The best way to hire a builder is to search out the most qualified and honest builder that you can find in your area. Then negotiate a fair price for the work. It is important to find someone experienced with antique homes and a passion for working on them. Builders who specialize in new houses are not necessarily qualified for a restoration project. The same goes for every subcontractor on the job.

The same is true for hiring the right architect. Don't pick the guy with the lowest fee. You want an architect who understands antique homes and is not going to transform your antique into something that looks like new. When interviewing architects, ask them if they have read this book.

Chapter Twelve
LEARNING YER Rs

Since colonial times, the three pillars of higher education have always been the three Rs—Reading, wRiting, and aRithmatic (but clearly not spelling). To fix up an antique home you must master a different set of Rs. Terms like renovation and restoration are often used interchangeably, but each has a very different meaning.

RENOVATION is fixing up an old house to make it more like a new house. In a typical renovation project, old windows are replaced with new vinyl-clad windows, crumbling plaster is replaced with drywall, the exterior is clad with vinyl siding to match the windows, bathrooms get new fixtures, and the kitchen gets a complete makeover. Not everything old is new again—architectural elements like doors, millwork, trim, and mantels that are in salvageable condition are stripped of paint and retained.

REMODELING is an extreme version of renovation. A remodeling contractor will nuke everything old, and when he is done you will think you are looking at a new house.

RESTORATION is taking a house back to the way it looked at some time in the past. It may mean taking it back to when it was first built or to some other time between then and now that is considered the significant period for the house. Later additions and alterations are removed and missing stuff is recreated.

REHABILITATION is fixing up a derelict house to make it livable or suitable for a contemporary use. Often it involves an adaptive reuse, such as converting a single-family residence to professional offices. Rehabilitation could include things like adding handicap ramps, egress stairs, sprinkler systems, and other building code requirements.

pRESERVATION is the repair and conservation of antique building elements. It does not take the house back to an earlier time but maintains the house in the here and now.

Antique house rehabilitated into professional offices.

Old windows are repaired and crumbling plaster is stabilized.

REPRODUCTION is building a replica of an antique house. It might be a replica of a house that once stood on the site, or it could just be a new house that looks just like an antique house. The houses at Colonial Williamsburg are mostly well-documented reproductions.

REINTERPRETATION is incorporating design elements from antique homes into a new home. The reinterpreted antique house is a hybrid that marries the best features of an antique home with the best design elements and technology of a new home.

REMUDDLING is a term coined by *Old House Journal* magazine. Every month they feature an example of a remuddled house that has been messed up so badly by inappropriate remodeling that it is both tragic and comic. Don't be a remuddler—nobody likes to be laughed at.

Now that you have learned the Rs of antique homes, it is time to move on to your next lesson.

Chapter Thirteen
RULES TO LIVE BY

If you obey all the rules you miss all the fun.

—Katharine Hepburn

I have always been a rules-are-meant-to-be-broken kind of guy, so it is odd for me to be writing about rules, but it is important to understand what the rules are so that you know when you are breaking them.

Secretary of the Interior Guidelines

The federal government has adopted guidelines for fixing up historic buildings. If you own a designated historic building, or if you want to cash in on historic tax credits, then the guidelines are rules that are rigidly enforced. For the rest of us, they are just suggestions.

1. A property shall be used for its historic purpose or be placed in a new use that requires minimal change to the defining characteristics of the building and its site and environment.
So if your antique house was originally built to be a single family residence, keep it that way if possible. That was an easy one.

2. The historic character of a property shall be retained and preserved. The removal of historic materials or alteration of features and spaces that characterize a property shall be avoided.
Don't remove any original historic fabric like doors, windows, or millwork. If the removal of something original to the house cannot be avoided, label it and save it—that is what the attic is for.

3. Each property shall be recognized as a physical record of its time, place, and use. Changes that create a false sense of historical development, such as adding conjectural features or architectural elements from other buildings, shall not be undertaken.
This is the rule that I just can't stop myself from breaking.

4. Most properties change over time; those changes that have acquired historic significance in their own right shall be retained and preserved.
With this rule I draw the line at the turn of the twentieth century. In particular, anything built after World War II is fair game for the dumpster

5. Distinctive features, finishes, and construction techniques or examples of craftsmanship that characterize a property shall be preserved.
I can't argue with this one.

6. Deteriorated historic features shall be repaired rather than replaced. Where the severity of deterioration requires replacement of a distinctive feature, the new feature shall match the old in design, color, texture, and other visual qualities and, where possible, materials. Replacement of missing features shall be substantiated by documentary, physical, or pictorial evidence.

Don't go replacing your tired old windows with new vinyl windows.

When digging around the site, keep an eye out for artifacts.

7. Chemical or physical treatments, such as sandblasting, that cause damage to historic materials shall not be used. The surface cleaning of structures, if appropriate, shall be undertaken using the gentlest means possible.

I did not heed this rule when I sandblasted the paint off the outside of my house thirty-five years ago. It was, without a doubt, the worst mistake I made.

8. Significant archeological resources affected by a project shall be protected and preserved. If such resources must be disturbed, mitigation measures shall be undertaken.

The ground around an antique house is full of buried artifacts. Old privy holes are an archeological treasure trove. When digging, be on the lookout. On a practical note, when I had a new septic system installed, it was all that I could do to keep the contractor from digging up my underground electrical service and killing every healthy tree on the site. I didn't have any luck getting him to watch out for pottery shards.

9. New additions, exterior alterations, or related new construction shall not destroy historic materials that characterize the property. The new work shall be differentiated from the old and shall be compatible with the massing, size, scale, and architectural features to protect the historic integrity of the property and its environment.

New additions must look similar to the original house, but not too similar. Good luck with this one.

10. New additions and adjacent or related new construction shall be undertaken in such a manner that if removed in the future, the essential form and integrity of the historic property and its environment would be unimpaired.

If you need to expand your house, build an addition alongside it. Don't tear off the roof and add another floor over the house. Most importantly, don't do anything irreversible.

My Rules

1. Repair or replace the building support systems first.
Before doing any cosmetic improvements to your house, address the support systems—electrical, plumbing, heating, insulation, and roofing. It may seem as though you are spending a lot of money and the house doesn't look any better, but if you don't deal with the building systems at the beginning of the project, it will cost a lot more to do them later and you will be tearing out new finishes to do the work.

2. Remove everything that doesn't look like an old house.
When Michelangelo was asked how he managed to carve the statue of David out of a block of marble, he replied that he just chipped away anything that didn't look like David. Restoring an antique house is the same idea—remove any modern finishes that don't look like they belong in an antique house.

3. Don't remove any original material.
Unless it is beyond repair and has turned into a moldy mass of rotted mush, don't remove anything that was original to the house.

4. Plumb, square, and level is not a realistic expectation.
You can level a house somewhat by jacking but you will never get it perfectly plumb, level, and square. Learn to live with it. If you can't, build a new house.

5. You don't have to live in a museum.
While it is important to respect the history of your home, you don't have to live like you are in the seventeenth century. It is okay to have central air-conditioning, flush toilets, and kitchen appliances.

6. Structural distress is not charming.
If your house is sagging and leaning due to structural deterioration or deficiencies, fix the structure. Repair the bug-eaten timber sills, rotted corner posts, and fractured timber joinery. Add some lally columns in the basement or whatever it takes to stabilize the structure. A structurally sound house can be charming too.

7. Don't mess with scale, proportions, or patina.
Don't even think about raising the roof, changing the window size and pattern, or adding dormers. You will ruin the antique character of the house.

8. Stick with natural materials.
You can't go wrong with wood, stone, or iron. There is no place for vinyl on an antique home.

Chapter Fourteen
SUSTAINABILITY

It's not easy being green.

—Kermit the Frog

It has been said that old is the new green. Restoring an antique house rather than tearing it down and replacing it with new construction is both a noble and sustainable undertaking. Building materials are conserved and carbon is sequestered from the atmosphere in the home's timbers.

But when it comes to energy efficiency, antique homes are at a serious disadvantage. They are seldom well-insulated and their heating systems are often functionally obsolete.

If we are to be good earthlings, it is obligatory that we insulate our homes and upgrade the mechanical systems as an essential part of any restoration and renovation project. To not do so is socially irresponsible.

Make your own electricity at home.

I have often heard historic preservation purists say silly things like, "you really do not need to insulate old houses—the way they built them years ago, they do not need insulation." My response is "hogwash!" Sustainability aside, you will never enjoy living in your antique home if you are not comfortable in it, and you will never be comfortable if your home is cold, damp, and drafty.

Sealing the Envelope

Insulating an antique house can be a challenge. Typically, wall cavities are only three inches deep and if the exterior walls are plank frame, there may be no cavity at all. The spacing between wall studs or attic joists seldom coincides with the standard widths of batt insulation. Worse yet, the wall cavity may already be filled with a primitive insulation such as bricks, newspaper, or corn cobs.

It is tempting to use spray urethane foam insulation, which conforms to irregular wall cavities and provides an airtight seal. But spray foams may not be the best choice for an

Insulating with spray foam.

Foil-faced insulation reflects heat when left exposed.

antique home. The biggest disadvantage is that spray foam insulation is irreversible—the foam sticks to everything it touches and you can never remove it.

My preference is cellulose insulation that can be blown into wall cavities and is environmentally friendly. If I make alterations in the future, I can always snake wires through the insulation or remove insulation that is in the way. It may not have as high an R-value as spray foam, but it is reversible.

It has long been believed that attics should be vented to the outside. Recent building science research has concluded that it is not a good idea after all. Attic vents bring cold, damp air into the house in the winter and admit hot, humid air in the summer. Heating and cooling equipment also works a lot harder when ductwork and air-handlers are in the attic.

In my own home, I have insulated below the roof rafters in addition to insulating the attic floor. I have removed the attic vents that I foolishly installed thirty years ago. The house is more comfortable in the winter and summer since I insulated the roof.

Venting crawl spaces to the outside is also not as good an idea as was once believed. Crawl spaces with earthen floors introduce a considerable amount of moisture into a home and adding vents to the outside only makes the situation

worse. It is a dirty job, but sealing the earthen floor with a vapor barrier and concrete slab is crucial. It is best to insulate the perimeter walls and vent the crawl space into the cellar rather than to the outside. I have found that spray urethane foam is the best insulation to use on the inside of a rubble stone foundation wall.

Antique homes are notorious for being drafty. It seems as though air leaks out everywhere you look. Air sealing to reduce infiltration is almost as important as insulating. Caulk everything that looks like a crack on the outside. On the inside, caulk below baseboards and inject expanding foam around electrical outlet boxes. Weather-strip doors and windows and make sure your fireplace dampers close tightly.

Many homeowners replace their antique windows with new windows unnecessarily. By adding storm windows to the outside, you can often achieve comparable energy performance at a fraction of the cost.

If you do a good job of insulating and air sealing, you may find that your fireplace no longer works the way it used to. A fireplace needs a massive amount of outside air leaking into the house to draw properly. If you find that your house fills with smoke when you light a fire, all you have to do is open a window and the fireplace will draw just like it used to, but that kind of defeats the purpose of trying to save energy.

A healthy home is a toxin-free home. Ridding your home of toxic materials requires a search and destroy effort.

Asbestos was a common ingredient in building materials manufactured between 1910 and 1980. It was used in pipe insulation, plaster, roofing felts, vinyl tile, cement board, and drainage pipe. Testing and remediation of asbestos is not a do-it-yourself project—get professional help.

Lead was a common pigment in oil-based paint from 1700 up to 1970. Breathing the dust from sanding paint containing lead can be hazardous to your health. While it is not absolutely necessary to remove all the old paint from your home, there are precautions that should be taken when working on painted surfaces.

If your home is heated with oil, chances are you have an underground storage tank. If the tank is more than thirty years old, there is a chance it has sprung a leak and is dumping oil into the ground. Not only is that a waste of good fuel oil, it can contaminate the groundwater. For my own home, I was able to switch to natural gas and eliminate the storage tank, but natural gas is not available everywhere.

Radon is a radioactive gas that occurs naturally in the ground from the decay of isotopes in the bedrock. Radon leaks out of the ground into your cellar through cracks in the floor slab and foundation walls. Crawl spaces with earthen floors invite radon into a home. In a drafty old home, the radon gas is quickly diluted and escapes into the atmosphere. Once you insulate and air-seal your home, you are now trapping and concentrating the radon gas inside. Radon vent pipes below the cellar floor that discharge through the roof are always a good idea.

Asbestos pipe insulation.

Some people have a sensitivity to certain molds, particularly candida mold. The mold spores are everywhere in the environment and it is not practical to try to eradicate them. Mold needs warmth, moisture, and a food source to flourish. Damp cellars and crawl spaces are havens for mold. The only practical way to control mold is to eliminate dampness.

Many modern building materials and furnishings can also introduce toxins into your home. Cabinetry and furniture made from particleboard composites can off-gas formaldehyde. Synthetic carpets and upholstery can also introduce toxins into the air. While it might feel homey for your house to have that new car smell, it really is not healthy. You can't go wrong with natural materials.

This antique home is within spitting distance of a busy state road and supermarket parking lot. It would be happier in the country.

Many antique homes are located in densely developed neighborhoods close to busy streets. There was not a lot of traffic when the house was built, but that cow path or wagon trail that wandered past the house evolved into an arterial roadway over the years. It is not uncommon to hear a homeowner lament, "I love my old house, but I wish I could just pick it up and move it to a different location." Actually, that is not as crazy an idea as it sounds.

A stone house on the move. *Courtesy of Wolfe House & Building Movers.*

Building-moving is not a new idea. It was actually somewhat commonplace in colonial times. When a new home was built, the old house would often be attached to the back as a kitchen ell or made into a barn. Teams of oxen would drag the house along a runway of wooden planks to its new home.

Today the tools are a little more advanced, but the process is much the same. We now have computer-synchronized hydraulic jacks and motorized dollies that make lifting and moving a house seem like child's play.

If you have a home that is poorly positioned on a site, maybe too close to the road or too close to a neighbor, it might be a candidate for relocation. If you have a failing foundation that must be replaced, it is often more practical to build a new foundation elsewhere on the site and move the house onto it rather than trying to rebuild the foundation under the house.

Moving a house is not as expensive as you might think, as long as you stay on the same site. It gets very pricey when you take it on the open road and have to start moving utility poles and streetlights.

Deconstruction and Reconstruction

If you want to move to a new neighborhood and take your house with you, deconstruction followed by reconstruction is the best strategy. A few years ago, I was involved in an exciting house relocation project. My client was the rock legend Daryl Hall. It turns out that Hall is not only an extraordinary guitarist, but he is also a connoisseur and collector of antique homes.

Hall acquired two derelict antique homes, one in Suffield, Connecticut, and the other in East Granby, Connecticut. Both homes had fallen on hard times. The Suffield house, built in 1768 by Oliver Hanchett, was a center hall Georgian home. Most recently, it had been used to house migrant tobacco farm workers. The tenants were also graffiti artists who did not seem to appreciate the architecture.

The house was carefully deconstructed piece by piece. *Courtesy of Analee Cole.*

The restored timber frame of the Bates Tavern. *Courtesy of Early New England Restoration.*

The two houses joined.

The Bates Tavern.

The East Granby house was a center chimney home built in 1774 by Lemuel Bates. It had once been a tavern and had been neglected for decades when Hall rescued it. The architecture was a little more primitive than the Hanchett house. It had few salvageable interior architectural features and much of the timber frame was badly rotted.

Both Hanchett and Bates were veterans of the American Revolution. The two houses were a few miles apart and had previously been related. Oliver Hanchett's daughter Rachel married Lemuel Bates' son. That the two houses were destined to come together was another one of those karma things.

Hall collaborated with architect Analee Cole to perfect a plan for transplanting the two houses to his ridgetop site in upstate New York, and joining them together. Every timber, floor board, door, and trim piece was painstakingly labeled and disassembled. Even foundation stones were moved.

The timber frame from the Hanchett house required only minor structural repairs, but the Bates tavern frame was in critical condition. It was rushed to the old house care center at Early New England Restoration in Pawcatuck, Connecticut, where it received reconstructive surgery. Each timber was meticulously repaired, patched, or replicated. The restored frame was assembled inside the shop and disassembled again before being released to its new home.

Barn-style timber frame connector between the relocated homes.

Chapter Sixteen
REINTERPRETING THE NEW ENGLAND HOME: THE NEW OLD HOUSE

If you have always dreamed of living in an antique home but cannot find one that suits your lifestyle, you are in luck—you can build your own. I know, it sounds too good to be true, but there is no reason why you cannot marry antique home design elements and materials with modern building technologies to create a new old house. You can site it wherever you like, have a floor plan that suits you, and incorporate energy-efficient technologies. The best part is, you don't have to deal with plaster dust, lead paint, or fossilized rodent feces. The trick is, you and your architect must be armed with a comprehensive understanding of antique home construction and design to pull it off successfully.

That is exactly what I did. In 2003 I purchased a ninety-one-acre wooded site in the Litchfield hills of northwestern Connecticut. I had spent over twenty years restoring and renovating my home in Westport and was ready for a different type of project. After some surgical land clearing and forestry management, I built a network of roads and a timber frame barn for a workshop. Then I embarked on building a reinterpreted antique New England saltbox.

Neighbors will often say things like, "Until you did the clearing I never realized that there was an old house back there," or "I really love your house—it looks like it has always been there."

Inside and out, the materials and details resemble an antique home, but below the surface lie structural insulated

My reinterpreted New England saltbox.

panels (SIPs), insulated concrete forms (ICFs), geothermal heating and cooling systems, and all of the modern conveniences that we have come to expect in a home.

Living room.

The key to a successful reinterpreted home is to stay true to a particular style and period. Don't start mixing elements from a first-period home with elements from a federal-period home. Of course, a reinterpreted New England home is really an updated rendition of a colonial revival, just done with a little more design sensitivity.

Dining room.

Master bedroom.

A brick patio looks more appropriate behind an antique home than a wood deck.

Part Three
BUILDING AND RESTORING

To really understand antique homes, it is not enough to just understand how they were built, you also have to understand the people who built them. I often hear people remark, "They sure don't build them like they used to," and I have to chuckle. The reality is that housewrights of days gone by were actually a lot like house builders today. A few were true craftsmen and took pride in their work, while most didn't much care. The homes that have survived as antiques are those built by the best craftsmen of their time.

Building a house is hard work, and the refreshment of choice among housewrights was hard cider. Building under the influence (BUI) was commonplace on construction sites. It is not hard to find examples of BUI even in the finest antique homes. But it is the little flaws and defects that, in an odd way, impart charm upon an antique home. You never hear anyone remark how charming it is that a home is plumb, level, and square. The flaws are a reminder that the home was built by hand, by imperfect mortals.

You must do a little deconstruction before you can begin construction.

Chapter Seventeen
EARTH, STONE, AND FIRE—MASONRY FIREPLACES, CHIMNEYS, FOUNDATIONS, AND OTHER HEAVY STUFF

The big fireplace below, inside, became now a place for a real fire.

—Frank Lloyd Wright

The landforms of New England have been transformed and sculpted by ice. Twenty thousand years ago, New England was invaded by a glacial ice sheet from Canada. All of New England became covered in a sheet of ice, nearly a mile thick, that scoured the land and bulldozed the soils into a big pile that became Long Island. When the ice eventually melted and the glacier retreated about 12,000 years ago, it left behind a thin coating of glacial drift on the scoured bedrock. The drift was a mishmash of boulders, rounded stones, sand, gravel, silt, and clay—bony soils referred to as glacial till. These glacial till deposits were a farmer's worst nightmare.

Connecticut hill town.

When the glacier retreated, the meltwater ran back to the sea through the Connecticut River Valley. A vast glacial lake formed in the river valley that stretched from south of Hartford to northern Massachusetts. In the still waters of the glacial lake, silt settled out in the summer, and clay settled out in the winter when the lake froze over. These banded silt and clay deposits, referred to as varved clays, accumulated to more than a hundred feet thick.

Where the glacial meltwater was able to flow directly to the ocean at Boston harbor and the coast of southern Maine,

blue marine clays were deposited. The varved clays of the Connecticut River Valley and the Boston blue clay became rich farm soils and also provided the raw material for brickmaking.

The glacier left behind a landscape of rolling hills that geologists refer to as glacial drumlins. Farmers built their homestead and towns on the hilltops, farmed the low field between the hills, and pastured their livestock on the slopes.

Part Three | Chapter Seventeen: Earth, Stone, and Fire—Masonry Fireplaces, Chimneys, Foundations, and Other Heavy Stuff

79

Cellar walls were made of fieldstone.

Chimney basement.

When building a house, the first order of business was to dig yourself a cellar hole. Every house needed a cellar to store vegetables and fruits where they would stay cool without freezing. The digging had to be done by hand and was back-breaking work. The cellar was only dug deep enough to comfortably stand up in. If the digging was particularly hard, the cellar would only extend under a portion of the house, and the rest of the house would have a crawl space. Despite the name, it was seldom deep enough to crawl into.

The cellar walls were built of fieldstone. The stones did not need to be gathered from far away. Often the stones dug out of the cellar hole were more than sufficient to build all of the foundations. The stone foundation for the chimney was called the basement and, as you might expect, the basement was in the cellar.

The cellar had an earthen floor that kept the house damp and moldy. In the early twentieth century it became trendy to cast a concrete floor slab in the cellar, but the slab was seldom more than two inches thick. The concrete floor made the cellar cleaner and drier. At the time, houses were being modernized to include electrical wiring, indoor plumbing, and central heat. These newfangled systems were located mostly in the cellar.

Even with a concrete floor, cellars tend to be wet spaces. When it rains, groundwater leaks through the joints between the wall stones and cascades down the cellarway stairs. Stone foundation walls are difficult to waterproof, particularly if the stones were dry laid without mortar.

Surgical excavation exposes rubble stone foundation.

Waterproofing and insulating the outside of a rubble stone foundation wall is a major undertaking. Unlike the inside of the wall, the outside face is typically very irregular with stones protruding. Earth was packed around the protruding

Chapter Seventeen: Earth, Stone, and Fire—Masonry Fireplaces, Chimneys, Foundations, and Other Heavy Stuff | **Part Three**

Cellarway.

To work in the crawl space, you have to pull up the floor boards.

stones as the wall was being built, making it difficult to dig alongside the foundation. Excavation must be done carefully to prevent the rubble wall from collapsing. Once the wall has been unearthed, it must be pressure washed and scrubbed to remove the soil stuck to the stones. A concrete wall then is cast against the stone wall. The concrete needs to be thick enough to encapsulate the protruding stones. You are now ready for the easy part: Apply a layer of foundation water-proofing and rigid insulation, install a footing drain, and backfill the whole mess with crushed stone. If this sounds like a lot of work, it is.

On my house, I have had some success plastering the inside of the cellar walls with stucco and then painting on a cementitious waterproofing. There is still some leakage during a heavy rain and the waterproofing has to be reapplied every few years, but it is still a lot better than it was before.

With an antique house, a bone-dry cellar is not a realistic expectation.

Cellarway stairs to the outside are always problematic. They provide an easy path for critters, criminals, and water to get into the house. Wooden cellarway doors always leak, and steel bulkheads never look right on an antique house. Whenever possible, it is a good idea to eliminate cellarways and block up the foundation wall. Interior stairs are a much more practical way of accessing the cellar.

Crawl spaces are nearly impossible to work in. It may sound extreme, but the most practical way to work in a crawl space is to carefully pry up the floorboards and work from above. It is usually the only way to seal the earthen floor with a vapor barrier and concrete slab. It is also the only way to repair or shore up the rotted or insect-damaged floor framing. This is a dirty job, but it has to be done.

Stone

Man has been building with stone since the stone age. In New England, there is no more plentiful building material than fieldstone. Sometimes called Connecticut potatoes, rounded, glacially deposited stone is the easiest crop to grow on a New England farm.

Fieldstone was used to build house foundations and stone fences. It actually takes considerable skill to build with rounded fieldstones that have few flat faces. It is like trying to stack marbles. Fieldstone fences were always dry-laid

without mortar. Very few stone masons have the skill to do that well.

In addition to having an over-abundance of fieldstone, New England is also home to some of the finest stone quarries in the world—granite, marble, brownstone, and slate. By the late eighteenth century, the tools and techniques to cut and shape stone became commonplace. It became fashionable to finish off the top of foundation walls with quarry stone. Sometimes the capstones are massive blocks of stone, other times they are just a thin veneer.

Dry-laid fieldstone wall.

Quarried capstone dresses up the foundation.

Slabs of quarry stone were used as exterior steps and stoops to finish off an entranceway. Brownstone used for stoops has been quarried in Portland, Connecticut, since the seventeenth century. The quarry has recently closed and is now home to a water park.

With all of that stone just laying around, you might expect to find a lot of stone houses in New England, but that is not the case. The early colonists came from a part of England with a tradition of timber frame construction and they just could not shake the habit.

The early English colonists also did not have the necessary skills to build a proper stone house. There is an account of an ill-fated attempt to build a stone house for Governor John Winthrop near Boston in 1631. Clay mortar was being used "for want of lime." Before the house was completed, a thunderstorm washed two of the walls down to the ground. The house was completed in timber.

Ironically, in Pennsylvania and New Jersey, German and Dutch settlers built many stone homes even though good building stone was hard to come by.

Brownstone entrance stoop.

Lime

Lime was a precious and scarce commodity in the early days. It was an essential ingredient of all things masonry. Mortar for brickwork and stone masonry was made from blending lime with sand. Plaster was also a blend of lime and sand with animal hair sometimes added for good mea-

Chapter Seventeen: Earth, Stone, and Fire—Masonry Fireplaces, Chimneys, Foundations, and Other Heavy Stuff | **Part Three**

Lime made by burning oyster shells in a lime rick. Colonial Williamsburg brickyard.

Lime putty.

sure. Whitewash paint was made from lime thinned with water.

Throughout most of the seventeenth century, the scarcity of lime forced masons to improvise. Foundation walls were built of dry-laid fieldstone. Brick chimneys were laid with clay mortar. Walls and ceilings were left unplastered.

At first, lime was made from oyster shells. The oyster shells would be burned on a hot wood fire, which converted the calcium carbonate (CaCO3) to calcium oxide (CaO), referred to as quicklime. The quicklime was then slaked by sifting it into tubs of water to convert it to calcium hydroxide (Ca(OH)2), referred to as hydrated lime. Slaking of lime is a violent exothermic chemical reaction that produces enough heat to make water boil. The slaking process could take several months to complete. The resulting hydrated lime took the form of a lime putty that was then ready for making mortar, plaster, or paint.

Lime became less scarce after deposits of limestone were found near Lincoln, Rhode Island. The limestone was burned

in kilns on a commercial scale. Marble deposits suitable for lime making were later found in northwestern Connecticut.

Modern mortars are made with Portland cement with lime added to improve workability. While cement-based mortars are harder and stronger than the old-style lime mortar, they are not necessarily better. Brick expands when it absorbs water and lime mortar will accommodate the movement. If an older brick wall is tuck pointed with a hard Portland cement mortar, the bricks will often shatter when they try to expand.

Portland cement mortar is gray in color and does not resemble an old-style lime mortar. If new brickwork is put in an antique house, it is a good idea to use a white Portland cement with a tan-colored sand to get a mortar color that looks right.

Brick

Brick homes never achieved the popularity in New England that they enjoyed in the South. In the southern colonies, clay suitable for brickmaking could be found everywhere. In New England, you had to look a little harder to find suitable clay deposits. They were mostly limited to places where glacial meltwater had accumulated. Brick homes were primarily confined to urban areas such as Boston where the

spread of fire was a concern. If you happen to stumble upon an antique brick home in the country, chances are the original owner had a fear of house fires.

Brick was used almost exclusively for building fireplaces and chimneys. A typical chimney consumed over 10,000 bricks. Some bricks were imported from England as ship ballast, but the ballast bricks were hardly enough to fill the

Part Three | Chapter Seventeen: Earth, Stone, and Fire—Masonry Fireplaces, Chimneys, Foundations, and Other Heavy Stuff

83

Brick homes are rare in the New England countryside.

Brick mold.

Bricks were fired in a clamp. Colonial Williamsburg brickyard.

Fired bricks were sorted into stock brick and common brick.

demand for chimney construction. A ship load of ballast brick was barely enough to build a single chimney and many of the ballast bricks were clinkers—reject bricks that had been badly distorted during firing.

The first large-scale brickmaking operation was in Medford, Massachusetts, north of Boston. Bricks were being made in Medford by 1660 and continued to be manufactured there by the New England Brick Company until 1912. Today, brick is manufactured in Bridgewater, Massachusetts, from clay deposited in glacial Lake Taunton.

The technology of brickmaking changed little over the centuries. Clay dug from the pit was blended with sand and water in an oxen-powered pug mill—a process called tempering. The tempered clay was then pressed into wooden molds and left outside to sun dry. The dried bricks were stacked to form their own kiln called a clamp. The clamp had a series of parallel tunnels where a wood fire would burn for several days to fire the bricks.

After the clamp had cooled down, the bricks were sorted. The hard-fired bricks closest to the fire, called stock brick, were a deep red or purple color. The softer bricks, called common brick, were a light salmon color. Only the stock brick was suitable for exposure to the weather and was reserved for the portion of the chimney exposed above the roofline. Common bricks were used on the inside of the chimney where they were not exposed to the elements.

Many people, in an effort to be authentic, make the mistake of purchasing used brick to rebuild a damaged chimney or for a garden path. Used brick is a random mix of stock brick and common brick. When exposed to the New England climate, the common brick will soon crumble and turn to dust. Modern bricks manufactured in New England look similar to historic bricks and are suitable for exposure to the elements. Some historic reproduction brick manufactured in the South are not able to withstand the New England climate but do just fine in Virginia and the Carolinas.

Chapter Seventeen: Earth, Stone, and Fire—Masonry Fireplaces, Chimneys, Foundations, and Other Heavy Stuff | **Part Three**

Fireplaces and Chimneys

The fireplace sat at the center of the home, both physically and socially. Everything happened at the fireplace hearth. That is where meals were cooked and where the family huddled for warmth in the winter.

The center chimney design was an example of Yankee ingenuity and practicality. By positioning the chimney in the center of the house, every room could have its own fireplace if it wanted one. In the winter, the brick masonry would heat up and radiant heat to the entire house with little heat lost to the outside.

The great fireplace is where meals were cooked. It was bigger than the other fireplaces in the home and was often tall enough to walk into. If the fireplace opening was too broad for an iron lintel to span, it would have a charred timber lintel, called a mantel tree, to support the brickwork above. It had an iron crane or lug pole to hang pots from and a beehive oven for baking. Cooking fires were kept burning night and day, year-round.

The beehive oven worked a lot like a modern pizza oven. The bricks surrounding the oven would be heated by a wood fire. When the bricks were hot enough, the hot coals and ash would be raked out of the oven, dinner or dessert would be put into the oven, and the door would be closed. Heat radiating from the brick would do the work.

In the early days, the beehive oven was located on the back wall of the great fireplace. Smoke from the wood fire would billow out of the oven door and be drawn up the fireplace flue. This arrangement proved hazardous for the women of the house who did the cooking.

Center chimney, Samuel Hartwell house site, Minuteman National Park, Lincoln, Massachusetts.

Part Three | Chapter Seventeen: Earth, Stone, and Fire—Masonry Fireplaces, Chimneys, Foundations, and Other Heavy Stuff

85

Walk-in great fireplace, with a beehive oven in the back and a mantel tree above. Parson Capen house, Topsfield, Massachusetts.

Beehive oven preheating.

Fireplace with the beehive oven and ashery on the side, Old Sturbridge Village.

Chapter Seventeen: Earth, Stone, and Fire—Masonry Fireplaces, Chimneys, Foundations, and Other Heavy Stuff | **Part Three**

Pots were hung from an iron crane. A cast iron fireback protected the brick from the heat of the fire. The loops on the andirons were for holding a roasting spit. The musket above the fireplace is a colonial revival fantasy.

Smoke oven for curing meats.

The chimney is not leaning; it was built that way.

Part Three | Chapter Seventeen: Earth, Stone, and Fire—Masonry Fireplaces, Chimneys, Foundations, and Other Heavy Stuff

87

T-shaped chimney on a saltbox house to accommodate an additional flue when the lean-to kitchen was added. Boardman house, Saugus, Massachusetts.

Attic roof hatch for putting out chimney fires.

The chimney was often the fanciest thing on a first-period home. John Ward house, Salem, Massachusetts.

Chapter Seventeen: Earth, Stone, and Fire—Masonry Fireplaces, Chimneys, Foundations, and Other Heavy Stuff | **Part Three**

They would need to step into the fireplace to tend the oven and, on occasion, their skirt would ignite. It is not known how many wives burned to death making dinner before someone got the idea of moving the oven off to the side of the fireplace and giving it its own flue.

To bake bread, the ash had to be cleaned from the floor of the oven, otherwise it would taint the bread. A flat piece of bread dough, similar to a pizza crust, would be placed in the oven. The resulting flatbread with the ash stuck to it was called cake. The cake was fed to servants and farm animals. Prior to the French Revolution, when Marie Antoinette was told that the people had no bread, she responded, "Let them eat cake." She was not referring to dessert cake.

The domed roof of a beehive oven was built by mounding up wet sand to support the brickwork. Once the mortar had set, the sand was dug out.

Directly below the oven was the ashery, where ash was stored. Wood ash contained potash (potassium), a valuable commodity. It was used as a fertilizer and for making lye soap. Potash was exported to England where it was in short supply since coal had replaced firewood as a fuel in many homes.

Many people have a notion that the proper place for the family musket or squirrel rifle was over the fireplace. In fact, that would have been a very foolish place to store a firearm. Not only is gunpowder and fire a dangerous combination, but the heat of the fire would have dried out the wooden gunstock. More likely, the rifle was stored over a doorway. The rifle over the fireplace is a fantasy born in the colonial revival era.

Some homes had a smoke oven in the belly of the chimney. Hams, bacon, and other meats would be hung inside the chimney to be cured by smoke from the fireplaces. The smoke oven would be accessed from a small door in the side of the chimney. The access door would be located in the attic or in the wall of the stair. Smoke ovens were considered a luxury and only the finest homes had one.

It was important for the chimney to penetrate the roof at the center of the ridge. Not only did it look good there, but it minimized roof leaks around the chimney. In many cases, the fireplace below did not align with the center of the ridge, so the chimney would be corbeled in the attic, giving the appearance that it was falling over.

While today it is a building code requirement for each fireplace to have its own flue, that was not always the case. Often all the fireplaces discharged into one central common flue. Having one large flue made it easy to clean the chimney. It was common practice to have a young boy climb up into the chimney to sweep it clean. As you might expect, chimney fires were common. Some attics had a roof hatch and ladder next to the chimney to facilitate putting out chimney fires.

Sir Benjamin Thompson a.k.a. Count Rumford, (1753–1814)

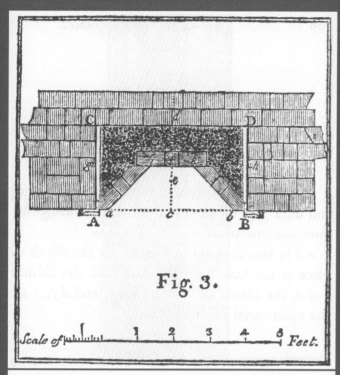

Drawing from Rumford's essay showing how to retrofit an inefficient firebox.

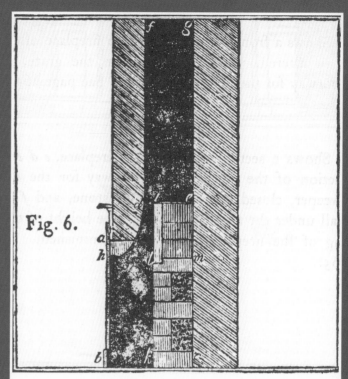

Drawing from Rumford's essay showing how to narrow the chimney throat.

Benjamin Thompson was a scientist, inventor, and sociologist. His scientific and intellectual accomplishments rivaled those of his contemporaries, Benjamin Franklin and Thomas Jefferson. Born in Woburn, Massachusetts, to a family of modest means, he had a talent for social climbing and charming men of power and influence.

At the ripe age of nineteen, he courted and married a wealthy older widow in Rumford, New Hampshire (later renamed Concord after the shot heard around the world). This catapulted Thompson into New England high society and an affluent circle of friends, including Governor Wentworth of New Hampshire.

He had a weakness for the ladies and could never pass up an opportunity to sleep with the wife of a friend or colleague. Consequently he managed to accumulate a number of powerful and influential enemies.

When the American Revolution broke out, Thompson remained loyal to the Crown. The governor awarded him a commission as a colonel in the loyalist forces fighting alongside the British. Although he never saw action, he was an effective spy for the British, which alienated him from

his patriot neighbors. Had he not backed the wrong horse, his later accomplishments would have filled American history books, but as fate would have it, he would only achieve fame in Europe.

In 1776, the British evacuated Boston, and Thompson went with them, leaving his wife and two-year-old daughter behind. He would never see his wife again and would not reconnect with his daughter for twenty years. Thompson took up residence in London, rubbed elbows with the upper crust, and soon befriended King George III, who knighted him for his services to the Crown as a spy.

Seeking a new adventure, in 1784 he traveled to Bavaria where he was appointed the minister of war. He reorganized the army and instituted social reforms. He got beggars off the streets of Munich and put them to work in factories where they learned a trade and received hot meals and a fair wage. The elector of Bavaria, Charles Theodore, made Thompson a count in 1791 in recognition of his accomplishments. He took the name Rumford from his former hometown in New Hampshire.

90

Chapter Seventeen: Earth, Stone, and Fire—Masonry Fireplaces, Chimneys, Foundations, and Other Heavy Stuff | **Part Three**

As a scientist, Rumford studied and experimented with the nature of heat. He proved that heat was a form of energy, not a substance. As an inventor, he developed, among other things, a more efficient cannon, invented the cooktop range, meat roaster, and coffee percolator.

One of his lesser accomplishments was his study of fireplaces and chimneys. In 1796, he published a long-winded essay titled "Chimney Fireplaces with Proposals for Improving Them to Save Fuel; to Render Dwelling Houses More Comfortable and Salubrious, and Effectually to Prevent Chimneys from Smoking." At the time, fireplaces where built deep and square with an oversized flue. They consumed copious quantities of fuel, were drafty, and downdrafts frequently filled the room with smoke.

Rumford's studies concluded that fireplaces should be shallow, with their sides splayed to radiant heat into the room. He also determined that the chimney throat should be made narrow to prevent smoke eddies and down drafts, and create a more efficient draft for the smoke. His essay included drawings showing how existing fireplaces could be modified to make them more efficient.

His work on fireplaces and chimneys was an overnight sensation. Fireplaces were retrofitted everywhere in London and it was not long before his ideas spread throughout Europe and America. Virtually all fireplaces built after 1800 followed Rumford's design.

By the second quarter of the nineteenth century, almost everybody was heating their homes with Franklin stoves rather than with their fireplaces, and Rumford's work was soon forgotten. With the colonial revival, fireplaces returned to fashion but were only used for romance, not for heating or cooking. Twentieth-century fireplaces were narrow and deep. They didn't work very well, but it didn't matter because they were seldom used.

Count Rumford had been all but forgotten in 1969 when Vrest Orton, the owner of the Vermont Country Store, wrote a short book titled *The Forgotten Art of Building a Good Fireplace*. He recounted Count Rumford's work on fireplaces and included his own drawings showing how a fireplace and chimney should be proportioned. Orton took some liberties with Rumford's work, and his drawings show the fireplace back sloping outward, which was not something that Rumford ever recommended, but nobody was the wiser. The book was a big hit and developed almost a cult following. Soon everybody, once again, wanted a Rumford fireplace in their home.

Spalled and crumbling brick has been pointed with Portland cement mortar.

Restored chimney with concrete-lined flues.

The chimney is the most tortured and abused part of any house. Where it peeks above the roofline, it is battered by snow, sleet, and rain. In the belly of its fireboxes, it is scorched by infernos that burn night and day. The inside of the flues are frosted with soot and flammable, corrosive goo and crud, where nesting birds and mischievous raccoons make themselves at home.

While roof shingles are only expected to survive exposed to the elements for a couple of decades, brick chimneys are expected to put up with the abuse for centuries. It is little wonder that we find them worn and weary.

The brickwork above the roofline will require repointing of the mortar joints every century or so. It is crucial that only a lime and sand mortar be used in the joints. If a Portland cement mortar is used, it could shatter the bricks and doom the chimney. If the bricks are loose or crumbling, the chimney may need to be rebuilt.

When I adopted my home, I found the brick chimney in pretty sorry condition. Four fireplaces and an oil-fired boiler shared a single flue. There was no flue liner and only a single thickness of brick separated the hot flue gases from the rest of the house. The bricks were turning to dust and oily creosote was oozing through the mortar joints and dripping down the face of the chimney. None of the fireplaces had dampers, so it was like having an open window in every room during the winter. It was evident that the chimney was unsafe and major work was needed; a simple fix would not do.

I took the chimney down to the floor of the attic and rebuilt it with new brick and copper step flashing at the roofline. I created separate flues for each of the fireplaces and the boiler with a concrete flue lining system. The flues were formed with rubber tubular bladders pumped up with air like balloons. A special lightweight refractory concrete was pumped into the chimney. When the concrete hardened, the forms were deflated and removed, leaving behind smooth, round flues. Unlike metal flues, the concrete bonds to the brick and reinforces the chimney structure. I don't have to worry about the flues rusting away, as the concrete will last forever.

I had custom dampers made for each fireplace by a steel fabricator. The dampers made the house a little more airtight and comfortable. As the crowning touch, I put a stone chimney cap on top to keep rain and snow out of the flues. A chimney cap is not necessarily historically correct, but it will extend the life of the chimney.

92

Chapter Seventeen: Earth, Stone, and Fire—Masonry Fireplaces, Chimneys, Foundations, and Other Heavy Stuff | **Part Three**

Chapter Eighteen
TIMBER FRAME

Raising a timber frame building is a magic moment. Weeks and months of hewing and sawing and boring and chiseling with nothing to show but a pile of numbered timbers culminate in just a few hours.

—Roy Underhill

For me, the timber frame has always been the most exciting part of an antique house or barn. With its massive hewn timbers and intricate handcrafted joinery, it has always reminded me more of fine furniture than of a structural frame. Nothing in a modern stick framed house comes close.

When I first started practicing engineering forty years ago, I would gaze in awe at antique house frames and marvel at the skill and craftsmanship that went into building them. I lamented that we could not build like that today. But now we can, thanks to a new generation of timber framers who have rediscovered the craft of timber framing that died out over a century ago.

The carpenters of days gone by left no written record of how they plied their trade. The skills they learned as apprentices to a master carpenter were trade secrets in the ancient tradition of the Old World craft guilds. But they did leave a record hidden in the surviving timber frames that they built. Today's generation of timber framers has studied the old frames—examining the tool marks, dissecting the joinery, and deciphering the layout marks. By trial and error, they have figured out how it was done and have mastered the old techniques.

Today's timber framers can not only reproduce the work of the old masters, they can do it better. To the early carpenters, building a house or barn frame was just a job. They only did as good a job as they had to. The carpenters who built barns were the ones that were not skilled enough, or

A flawless timber frame. *Courtesy of New England Timber Framers.*

sober enough, to build house frames. To today's timber framers, crafting a flawless timber frame is a passion.

Timber framers today also have the benefit of modern engineering. While timber framers were busy rediscovering the craft, a small, core group of structural engineers were hard at work figuring out how to apply engineering principals to the design of traditional timber structures. It has been a high point of my professional career to have been a part of that effort.

The Trees

The vast New England forests provided the early housewrights with what seemed to be a limitless supply of raw materials. Timbers were hewn or sawn from trees harvested on the site. Oak was the preferred timber because that was what had been used to build frames in Old England. But they were not the same oak trees; they were tall and straight forest-grown trees, unlike the field-grown trees of England that were short and sprawling.

The timbers in first-period homes were massive because large, old-growth trees were easy to come by. By the mid-eighteenth century, the forests had been cleared for farming and old growth oak trees were harder to find. The size of timbers used to build frames slowly diminished as time went on, and other trees besides oak were finding their way into house frames—whatever timber was most readily available on site.

There is a notion that early New England forests were dominated by white pines. That is actually not true. One of the reasons for this notion is that accounts from early colonists often referred to pine forests, but the early colonists were not educated in botany. They referred to all conifer trees as pines and all shore birds as ducks.

By studying fossilized tree pollen buried in bogs, scientists have been able to determine what species of trees were growing in New England when the first Europeans arrived nearly 400 years ago. What they discovered is that the mix of tree species growing then was similar to the trees growing today. The forests of northern New England were dominated by conifers—predominantly spruce and pine with a few hemlocks and firs. The forests of southern New England were dominated by hardwood trees—predominantly oak and chestnut with some maple and hickory. Massachusetts was somewhere in the middle and hosted a mix of conifer and hardwood forests.

Forest-grown oak trees grow tall and straight, reaching for the sun.

Low-impact logging. Courtesy of New England Timber Framers.

A round log converted to a square timber with nothing but an axe.

A hewn timber face is smoothed with a broad axe. *Courtesy of Jack Sobon.*

If trees were square rather than round, it would be a lot easier to build buildings out of them; but unfortunately, they don't grow in that shape. So once the trees had been felled, the next order of business was to convert them to square timbers.

The ancient, time-honored method of timber conversion is hewing with axes. The log is hewn flat, one side at a time. A series of notches are chopped in the side of the log with a felling axe and then the wood between the notches is split away. The face of the log is then hewn to a roughly flat surface with a broad axe. After two opposing faces have been hewn flat, the log is rotated ninety degrees so that the final two faces can be hewn. It sounds pretty easy, but in fact, it is back-breaking work.

In early frames, all of the timbers were hewn. As time went by, only the larger timbers in a frame were hewn and the smaller timbers were sawn. Hewing was a common activity up until the mid-nineteenth century.

The earliest method of sawing timbers and boards was pit sawing. The log to be converted would be laid across a trench or pit and sawn with a two-man saw—the sawyer, standing on top of the log, and the pitman, standing in the pit. In New England, pit sawing was only practiced in the seventeenth century, while in the southern colonies it was practiced into the late eighteenth century. Once water-powered sawmills were built, New Englanders had no use for a pit saw. In the South, the scarcity of suitable water mill sites, and the

Pit saw.

availability of slave labor, made pit sawing more popular. It is rare to find a pit-sawn timber or board in a New England home.

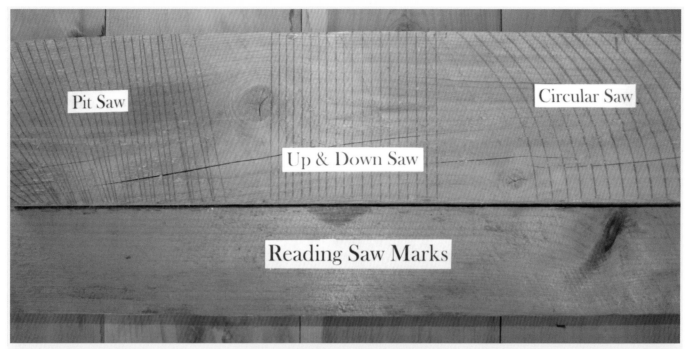

Saw marks tell a story.

Water-powered sawmills were built very early in New England. The first recorded sawmill was built in 1633 at the Falls of the Piscataqua River, near Portsmouth, New Hampshire. There was no shortage of suitable sites for water-powered mills. When a new township was established, one of the first structures built was a sawmill. Prosperous towns had two or three sawmills.

The saw was held in a wooden frame called a sash. The saw would move up and down in a reciprocating motion as the log was advanced by a cog wheel. The up and down action of the saw emulated a man-powered pit saw. The rotary motion of the water wheel was converted to an up and down motion by a mechanical arm called a pitman in honor of its human ancestor. The sawing process was slow since the saw only cut on the down stroke and did nothing particularly useful on the up stroke. But it still beat the pants off of a pit saw.

Rotary circular sawmills did not become popular in New England until after

Up and down sawmill, Shelburne Museum.

TIMBER NOMENCLATURE

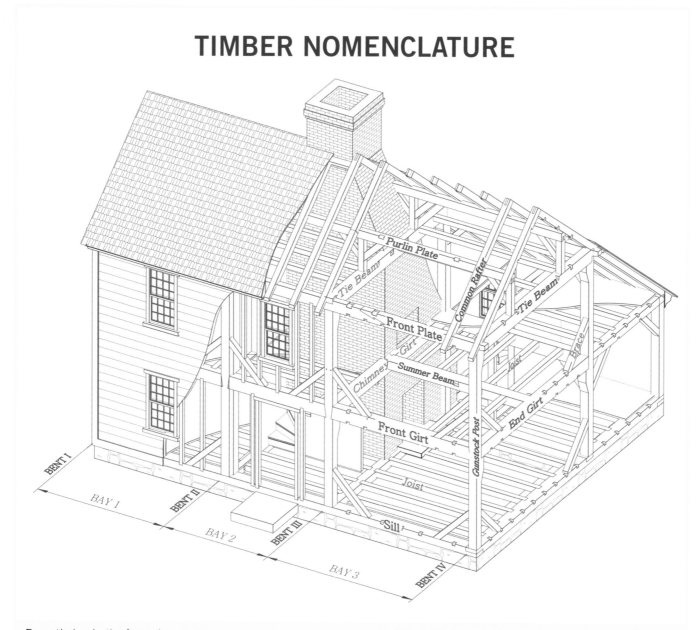

Every timber in the frame has a name.

1830. When hitched to a steam engine, a circular saw could cut wood considerably faster than a water-powered up and down mill.

By examining the saw marks on a timber, it is easy to determine what kind of saw was used to cut it. The saw marks left by an up and down sash saw are parallel and evenly spaced. The saw marks from a pit saw are more irregular and not exactly parallel. A circular saw leaves characteristic curved saw marks. A modern bandsaw mill leaves saw marks similar to a water-powered up and down saw.

A modern bandsaw mill. Courtesy of New England Timber Framers.

The Frame

Early New England timber frames were built in the tradition of medieval English frames. The configuration of the timbers and the joinery were distinctively English and unlike the Dutch frames of the Hudson River valley, the German frames of Pennsylvania, or the French frames of Quebec. Over time, the frames evolved to a distinctively American style. Medieval design elements such as jetties fell out of fashion, joinery became less complex, and more efficient methods of laying out the joinery were developed.

First-period frames were intended to be on display. Timbers were planed smooth and embellished with decoratively carved chamfers, gunstock posts, and finials or drops. A century later, lime was readily available for making plaster and it was no longer fashionable to expose the frame. Concealed behind plaster ceilings, the timbers were left rough cut. Where exposed in attics and cellars, timbers were left in the round with the bark in place and were sawn flat on the top surface only. It would be another two centuries before architecturally exposed timber frames were celebrated.

The framing layout for a center chimney home was somewhat predictable. The frame would be three bays wide, with the center bay narrower than the side bays and consumed by the chimney and stair.

The Summer

A summer beam with an ovolo chamfer and lamb's tongue stop.

Exposed summer beam.

One of the defining elements of an English frame was the summer beam. The summer was a stout timber in the first floor ceiling that spanned the width of each of the side bays. It supported the second-floor joists and was supported by the chimney girt and the end wall girt. Because of its massive size and prominence in the middle of the room, it is an often admired and celebrated timber. The name is not a reference to the season of the year; it is derived from the Norman French word for pack horse, *sommier*.

Architectural historians, uneducated in the basic principles of structural engineering, will often pontificate on the great strength of the summer beam holding up the floor. In fact, from a structural engineering standpoint, the summer beam makes no sense at all. It would be far more efficient, and stronger, if the summer beam had been eliminated and the floor joists spanned directly to the chimney girt and end girt. Interestingly, that is exactly the way the first floor and attic floor were typically structured—the summer beam was often only found at the second floor.

To make matters worse, the summer was supported at the mid-span of the chimney girt and end girt, which was their weakest point. Furthermore, the girts were significantly weakened at their point of maximum stress by the wood removed to create the summer beam joint. Many of the structural failures I have observed in antique homes happen where the summer and end girt are joined.

So if the summer beam wasn't such a good idea, why did they do it in the first place? If you could go back in time and ask the carpenters, they would probably reply, "That is the way that it has always been done." If you were to go back further, to medieval England, and look at the timber frames being built, you would find the answer. To create a jetty on the front of a house, the second-floor joists had to be oriented perpendicular to the front wall so that they could cantilever. Since the floor joists could not span all the way to the back wall, a summer beam was needed to support the joists.

When jetties on the front of homes fell out of fashion, the summer beam could have faded into the sunset, but carpenters kept on building the way they had been taught without questioning. It would take another century before summer beams passed into extinction.

Floor joists cantilever to create a jetty.

Roof Framing

There were a few variations in the way timber roofs were framed. They were either common rafter or common purlin configurations. Rafters are the timber that span up the slope of the roof and purlins span across the slope. Common timbers are spaced between two feet and three feet apart and make up the majority of the roof timbers. Commons were supported by principal timbers or plates. If a horizontal timber stands up straight rather than being inclined with the roof slope, it is called a plate.

Very often, I will find timber roof framing for an antique home that is undersized and structurally deficient. It is usually evident from a casual glance at the roofline. It is not even necessary to climb up into the attic to see that there is a structural issue. If the roof is sagging and deflected, the

Common rafter and principal purlin roof.

Common purlin and principal rafter roof.

A rocking and rolling roof structure is experiencing structural distress. Fairbanks house, Dedham, Massachusetts.

This barn has fallen on hard times.

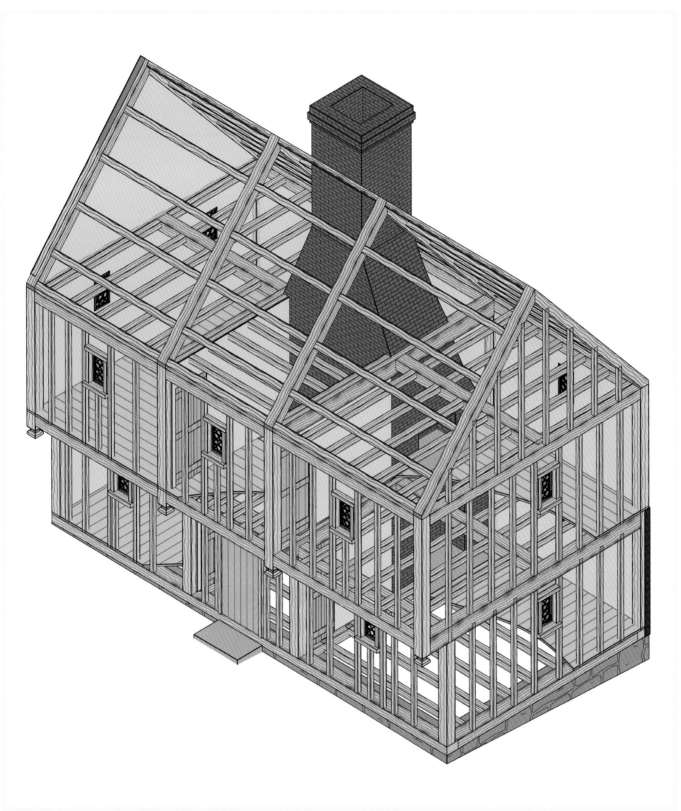

Timber frame of a first-period house with a common purlin and principal rafter roof.

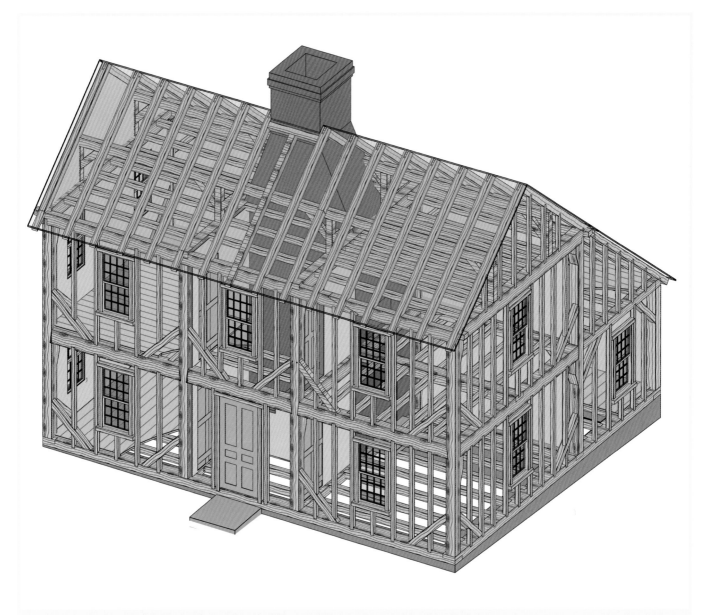

Timber frame of a saltbox with a common rafter and purlin plate roof.

structure is in trouble. It is not charming and contrary to popular belief, it is not supposed to be that way.

The thing that saves many homes from collapse is the total lack of insulation in the attic. In the winter, the heat loss through the roof will melt the snow on the roof before it can accumulate. If the home is insulated as part of a renovation project, the weight of the additional snow on the roof could have dire consequences. I am not advocating that antique homes not be insulated, that would be irresponsible. What I am suggesting is that if your roof framing is exhibiting signs of structural distress, deal with it.

Persistent roof leaks that are ignored can also have serious consequences. If the timbers are allowed to stay wet, it does not take long for rot to set in. This is a common problem with old barns. In much of New England, farming was no longer a viable livelihood by the early twentieth century. When barns were no longer needed to house animals and crops, maintaining their roofs became a low priority. By the time a homeowner decides to fix up that old barn out back, he is often several decades too late. It is sad to see once proud old barn timbers reduced to a pathetic mass of soggy mush.

The craft of timber framing is all about the joinery—fitting the timbers together with intricately cut joints. If the wrong type of joint is selected for a particular application, or if it is carelessly cut, the timbers will not fit together on raising day, or worse yet, may not perform under service conditions.

Several regional styles of timber framing have evolved over the ages, each with its own vocabulary of joints. English-style joinery predominated in New England, for obvious reasons, and was distinctly different from Dutch, German, or French timber frame joinery practiced elsewhere in the New World. While the time-honored English traditions were respected, a distinctive American style of timber framing soon evolved.

Dozens of timber joints were commonly used in English frames, each with a specific application and its own odd name. Many were variations on inserting a square tenon into a square hole, called a mortise, and securing the joint with wood pegs, called treenails. While cutting a tenon with a series of saw cuts is somewhat straightforward, cutting a square mortise hole is not as simple. Until recently, there was no tool that could drill a square hole, so you started by drilling a series of round holes and then squaring off the mortise with sharp chisels.

The treenails, sometimes also called trunnels, were made from riven hardwood and had a gradually tapered, blunt point. The holes to accept the treenails were slightly offset between the mortise and the tenon. This was called draw boring. When the treenail was driven through the draw bored holes, it pulled the joint together and held the joint tight when the timbers dried.

Laying out joinery is pretty simple if all the timbers are perfectly straight and cut to consistent dimensions. Unfortunately, timbers hewn with axes or sawn with a water-powered mill were seldom straight and rarely of uniform dimension. A method for laying out joinery with imperfect timbers was needed. The method that had been perfected over thousands of years was called the scribe rule. Timbers would be arranged in their intended configuration on the floor of the shop and stacked and leveled, one over the other. Using plumb bobs, the dimensions of one timber would be projected onto its intended mate. The mortise would then be cut in one timber and a short tenon would be cut in the other. The joint would then be assembled and the profile of the mortise timber would be scribed onto the tenon timber with a pair of dividers. The joint would then be taken apart and the cutting of the tenon would be completed to the scribed line. Each timber was then marked with chisel-cut Roman numerals, called marriage marks, so

A square rule mortise. *Courtesy of New England Timber Framers.*

An English tying joint. *Courtesy of New England Timber Framers.*

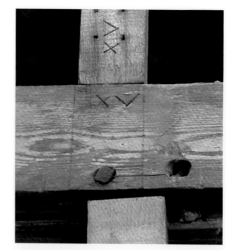

Marriage marks.

TIMBER JOINERY

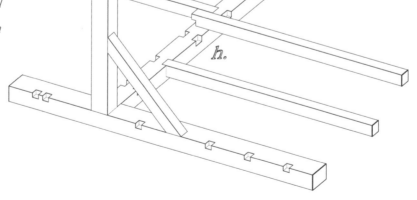

a. – Bridle
b. – English tie joint
c. – Scarf
d. – Step lap seat
e. – Housed Dovetail
f. – Soffit Tenon
g. – Mortise & tenon
h. – Butt Cog

Common timber joints in an English-style frame.

For scribe rule joinery, the timbers are first stacked on each other in their final configuration. *Courtesy of New England Timber Framers.*

A square rule joint. The blue lines delineate the perfect timber hiding inside.

that they could find the right mate on raising day. As you might imagine, the scribe rule was very labor intensive.

There had to be a better way, and with a little Yankee ingenuity, a better method of laying out joinery was found. It became known as the square rule method. The square rule was based on the principal that within every imperfect timber exists a slightly smaller, perfectly straight, uniform timber. At the location of a joint, each mating timber would be reduced to the dimension of the imaginary perfect timber. Joints could then be cut without ever putting the timbers together until raising day. If there were multiple similar timbers in the frame, the timber parts could be interchange-

able. For instance, all of the rafters or all of the knee braces could be interchangeable and would fit anywhere in the frame. By using the square rule method, a timber frame could be cut in less than half the time of the scribe rule method.

The first documented square rule timber frame was built in 1801 and carpenters were quick to adopt the new method. The old scribe rule method was cast aside without a tear being shed. Since it is easy to identify a square rule frame by examining the joinery, it is a house dating tool. It is impossible for a square rule timber frame to have been built prior to 1801, regardless of what the plaque out front says.

Studs and Planks

Exterior walls were typically framed with vertical 3×3 timber studs spaced approximately two feet apart. The ends of the studs fit loosely into mortises cut into the sills and girts. The studs were slender timbers that were not intended to be load-bearing. They were only there to provide something to nail the siding and plaster lath to. But invariably, they were pressed into service as load-bearing posts when the timber girts above deflected or sagged under the load from the summer beam.

If you decide to replace the plaster in your home with drywall, you may live to regret it. The studs were set at an irregular spacing and were rough sawn to inconsistent dimensions. Plasterers adjusted for the variations in the studs by varying the thickness of the plaster. Drywall sheets will not lay flat across the studs. The walls will first need to be painstakingly cross-furred and shimmed before hanging the drywall.

Occasionally, homes were built without any studs in the exterior wall. Instead, two-inch-thick, vertical oak planks were attached to the outside of the timber frame. The planks were two stories tall and ran continuous from the sills to the roof plate. They were secured to the timbers with treenails and rested on a rabbet cut in the top of the sill timber. The exterior siding and the plaster lath were nailed directly to the planks. Not surprisingly, these homes were called plank frame homes.

On some plank frame homes, the timber posts were cut out after the planks were in place. This was done so that there would not be any bump outs on the inside of the wall where the posts had been. The planks thus became load-bear-ing and were holding up the timber frame. Extreme caution should be observed when making openings in a plank frame wall.

Plank framing is a renovator's worst nightmare. There is no wall cavity to insulate and no place to run electrical wiring, plumbing pipes, or anything else. The only practical option is usually to stud the wall out after removing the plaster, wainscoting, and any other interior finishes. Window jambs, doorways, and cased timbers have to be reworked. Naturally, all of this will alter the look of the space and historic accuracy must be sacrificed for the sake of practical utility.

Frame Raising

Raising day was exciting. The skeletal frame rose into the air in a single day, and what had been a muddy hole in the ground suddenly looked like a house. Many people have a romantic image of an Amish raising bee, with a swarm of men in straw hats, beards, and suspenders, pushing massive timber bents into the air with pike poles, while the women folk cooked up a feast, served lemonade, and sewed quilts. Certainly that sort of festive frame raising did happen now and then, but not very often. Usually it was a small crew of carpenters raising the frame, without fanfare or celebration. They used gin poles to lift the heavy timbers the same way that we use hydraulic cranes today.

Timber frames today are erected primarily with cranes.

The frame raising culminated with the "topping out" as the last roof timbers were hoisted into position with a pine bough nailed to the peak. The topping out tradition is an ancient Scandinavian, pagan custom that dates to 700 AD. According to legend, the ritual appeased the forest gods for having taken the trees from them, in the hope that the gods would not take revenge against the home by cursing it with bad luck. It was more civilized than the earlier Roman custom of appeasing the forest gods with a human sacrifice.

Topping out is celebrated with a conifer bough secured to the peak of the roof.

Lifting timbers into place with a gin pole equipped with a block and tackle. *Courtesy of Jack Sobon.*

Decline and Rebirth

The industrial revolution was not kind to the ancient craft of timber framing. A few technological developments would spell the demise of the time-honored tradition.

The circular saw came into common use around 1830. All of a sudden, uniform dimension lumber such as 2×4s, 2×6s, and 2×8s could be produced quickly and inexpensively. By 1840, railroads were being built across the land and lumber could be transported from western forests to the urban centers in the East. The third development and figurative coffin nail of timber framing was the machine-made nail.

By the start of the Civil War, houses were being built from dimension lumber nailed together rather than from timbers. This new type of wood framing was called balloon framing by the old-time carpenters. They claimed that the framing was so light that it would just blow away like a balloon. But they didn't blow away and balloon framing proved to be a quicker and cheaper way to build than timber framing. More significantly, it allowed homes to be built with less skilled carpenters, and skilled workers were in short supply. By the end of the nineteenth century, only barns, mills, and bridges were being built of timber and by the early twentieth century, there were no timber frame carpenters left. It seemed as though timber framing was gone forever, but it would rise from the ashes.

In the 1970s, winds of change were blowing through the American building industry. There was a growing dissatisfaction with the sterile and characterless nature of postwar homes. A grassroots movement to return to hand-built homes began to gain momentum. Simultaneously, another grassroots movement to build more energy-efficient homes was gaining traction. These two groups collided head on and merged into the alternative building technology movement. These were exciting times for building and, as a young engineer, I was swept up into the effort to explore and experiment with new technologies like solar energy.

One branch of the alternative building technology movement was the timber frame revival—the rediscovery of the lost craft of timber framing. A handful of craftsmen, working out of barns and garages in the woods of New England, were taking apart old barn frames and figuring out how the old-timers did it. They experimented with chisels and axes,

Super-sized power tools. *Courtesy of New England Timber Framers.*

Automated timber cutters make quick work of fabricating precisely cut timber structures.

hacking timber frames out of trees until they were able to reproduce the work of the old masters.

The historic preservation movement was underway at the same time. Urban homesteaders were buying derelict, old, inner-city homes and fixing them up. They defied the trend of the times to tear down blighted neighborhoods and build high-rise apartment projects.

At the time, the alternative building technology movement was not a part of the mainstream construction industry. Architects and contractors believed that they were just a bunch of stoned-out old hippies. If they just ignored them, they would fade away, but that did not happen. The timber frame revival and the historic preservation movement were destined to thrive and overtake the mainstream.

The alternative energy movement was not as fortunate. The goliath oil and nuclear industries proved too powerful to beat and the movement eventually ran out of steam. It went underground for a couple of decades until the ideas were rediscovered by a later generation that coined the term, "sustainability," and pretended that it was a new idea they had just discovered.

The timber frame revival got a boost in 1989 when *This Old House* reconstructed a timber frame barn on national TV. Viewers who had never seen timber framing before sud-

denly wanted to live in a hand-crafted timber frame home. Within a few years, timber framing companies that had been struggling were transformed into factory operations with German-made CNC fabricating equipment. The timber frame revival had matured and entered the world of mainstream construction. The old craft was back and it was here to stay, but it would never be the same.

Today, timber framing is a vibrant and diverse building industry. There are traditionalists following historical forms and using historic hand tools. Small timber frame shops are building contemporary timber frames using specialized power tools, and there are a number of successful factory fabricators producing large-scale timber frame buildings with automated, computer-controlled equipment. It is ironic that the timber frame revival that was born from a desire for hand-crafted homes is now a technologically sophisticated industry.

"Trimber" Framing

Not all timber frames built today actually hold anything up. It has become fashionable to erect non-structural timber framing inside a house as pure decoration. The timbers are essentially super-sized architectural trim. This is referred to as trimber framing.

I used to have a negative attitude about trimber. I believed it was a fraud and diminished the dignity of the craft. In my old age, I have become more tolerant and less idealistic. If it gives people pleasure to have trimber framing in their home, then why not?

Trimber truss. *Courtesy of New England Timber Framers.*

Trimber frame master bedroom.

A few years ago, I renovated the master bedroom in my home. The master bedroom is in a wing of the house that was built in 1930 and lacked any Old World character—so I went trimber. Some may think that I sold out, but I love the way it turned out. Joe Turco of New England Timber Framers did a masterful job of crafting the trimber out of some weathered white oak that he had lying around his yard. The only problem is that it came out looking better than the authentic timber framing in the house.

Fungus, Bugs, and Other Creepy Stuff

Wood is an organic material grown out of the earth, and the forces of nature are forever at work, diligently trying to return it to the earth. It takes human effort to keep a timber structure from meeting its inevitable fate.

Dry rot is a fungus that, despite its name, only consumes wet timber. Rot fungus requires food, warmth, oxygen, and water to flourish. If you deny it water, you can keep it at bay. But if you ignore persistent roof leaks, the fungus will win the battle and slowly consume your home or barn. Once rot fungus has consumed ten percent of the mass of a timber, which is barely perceptible, the timber will have lost as much as eighty percent of its structural strength. It doesn't take long before the situation becomes critical.

Termites, like rot fungus, also like to dine on wood. But they seldom eat at home. Termites live in subterranean cities called colonies, and they prefer to eat out. They travel in tunnels to your home to dine on your timbers and then return to their colony after they have had their fill. They have a sophisticated society that you don't expect from bugs. They

Rotted corner post.

Joe Turco, Master Timber Framer and Joiner

Joe Turco of New England Timber Framers is an extraordinary craftsman. His hand-crafted frames are works of art. He never passes up a challenge and always finds a way to do what others thought to be the impossible. He gives new meaning to the term "Yankee ingenuity." But what he is best known for is his big grin and his knack for keeping everybody laughing.

Joe Turco drilling out a mortise.

Termite-damaged post base.

Powder post beetle–damaged floor joist.

Termite bait station.

have a royal ruling class, working-class termites, and an army of soldiers. Like vampires, termites cannot stand the light of day. They will hollow out a timber but seldom break through to the surface. Their affinity for the dark makes them seem even more sinister. The subterranean termites that inhabit New England are less industrious than their relatives living in tropical climates. While tropical varieties can consume a house in a few short years, subterranean termites will take a century to do the same amount of damage. When termites are found in an antique home, they are usually low to the ground. They generally confine their dining to the first-floor framing and the bottoms of posts. They just don't like climbing stairs. If you find termites in the attic, then you are in serious trouble. They only climb that high if there is nothing left to eat downstairs.

Unlike termites, carpenter ants don't eat wood, but they do like to live in it. They prefer to eat the crumbs of food that you leave on the kitchen floor, and they hate the taste of wood. Carpenter ants are cave dwellers that excavate tunnels in wood for their nests. You will often find little piles of sawdust that they have discarded from the tunnels. They

prefer to live in wet, partially decayed wood. So if you find a nest of carpenter ants, you probably had a problem before they moved in.

The most pervasive and destructive bug in an antique timber home is not the termite or carpenter ant, it is the powder post beetle. It is rare to find an antique house that does not have some powder post beetle damage. They are usually only found in the first-floor framing and typically only dine on the sapwood of hardwood species. They particularly like the taste of oak. Powder post beetles will sneak into a house as stowaways, hiding under the bark of timber joists when the house was built. Beetles will spend their entire life burrowing through wood, eating as they go, and leaving behind fine, powdery frass the consistency of flour. Frass is a polite word for bug turds. When they reach adulthood, they emerge from the wood, leaving a pinhole on the surface. They lay their eggs on the surface, and the next generation follows in the footsteps of their parents. For the beetles to survive, the wood must have moisture. They die of thirst in dry timbers, but in a damp cellar or crawl space, conditions are ideal, especially if there is an earthen floor.

Now that you understand your enemies a little better, you are ready to wage war against them. First priority is to dry everything out. Fix the roof, siding, downspouts, and flashings. Make sure that water drains away from the house and don't let the siding come close to touching the ground. Cut down any shrubs that touch the house.

If you have a cellar or crawl space with an earthen floor, put down a vapor barrier and pour a concrete slab over it. If the cellar is still damp, plug in a dehumidifier.

Next, make your timbers taste bad to fungus and bugs. Spray exposed timbers with a borate solution. Borate is not toxic to humans or pets, but bugs hate it.

If you have active termites, destroy their cities. Termite colony elimination involves luring termites into bait stations planted around the house. The traps are baited with pieces of wood, and when termites take the bait, poisoned bait is substituted for the wood in the trap. The worker termites will take the poisoned bait back to their city and feed it to their friends. This may sound sneaky, but this is war!

Timber Restoration

Inevitably, the bugs and fungus will win a few battles and inflict wounds on your timbers. Epoxy fillers and consolidants can be effective at healing deteriorated wood that is not structural, such as window sills. But badly deteriorated structural timbers will probably have to be amputated and undergo reconstructive surgery.

The most vulnerable timbers are the sills that rest on the foundation. They are the closest timbers to the ground and the first place that termites and rot fungus will attack. If you are lucky, the sill deterioration will be isolated to a few small areas that can be cut out and patched. If you are not so lucky, you may need to jack up the structure and replace large sections of sill timber.

Post bases are also vulnerable to deterioration and will frequently need to have a new post base spliced in. When patching timbers, a combination of structural adhesives and high-strength screws are used to bond the old wood to the new. Epoxy and urethane adhesives work well. Construction adhesives that come in a caulking tube are not structural adhesives and are not suitable for timber restoration work.

Wood used for patching timbers should be of a similar species. Don't try bonding softwoods to hardwood timbers. The new wood also needs to have a similar moisture content as the old timber. Otherwise, the patch will self-destruct when the wood dries and seasons at a different rate. Reclaimed antique timber works best. If the repaired timber

Timber sill replacement. *Courtesy of Early New England Restoration.*

Replacement of timber end girt. Thomas Lee house, East Lyme, Connecticut. *Courtesy of Early New England Restoration.*

A restored barn frame for a new home on a ridgetop in Salisbury, Connecticut.

will be exposed to view, you will need to also match the surface texture of the old wood. For instance, you may need to hew the face of the patch if the old timbers were hewn.

Repairing and patching deteriorated timbers in place can be difficult and costly. With barn frames, it is usually more practical and cost-effective to dismantle the frame, repair the timbers in a shop, and re-erect the frame on a new foundation.

Chapter Nineteen
ROOFING AND SIDING

If the timbers are the bones of the house, the roofing and siding are the skin that protects the house from the elements. When the Old World, traditional materials proved unsuited to the New World climate, New Englanders adapted and improvised. Thatched roofing and wattle and daube walls gave way to wood shingles and clapboards. A distinctively American architecture was in the making.

At first, riven oak was used for roof shingles and clapboards. In fact, the term clapboard is derived from the German word *klappholt* for a riven oak barrel stave. Oak was a familiar material to English carpenters and was easy to split, but it was not decay resistant and proved to be a poor choice for exterior cladding. Eastern white pine soon became the dominant wood species for roofing and siding. It was slightly more durable than oak, but not ideal. Eastern white cedar is a naturally decay-resistant wood species that eventually became the preferred material for roofing shingles where it was available. Since eastern white cedar grows primarily in Northern New England, it was not available everywhere.

Roofing

Wood shingles were the roofing material of choice in early New England and they are usually the most appropriate roofing material for an antique home today. Wood shingles are more costly and require more maintenance than asphalt shingles, but they look a whole lot better.

Wood roofing shingles today are made from western red cedar, which is significantly more decay resistant than the wood species available to early New Englanders. It would be foolish to reroof an antique home today with pine shingles for the sake of historical authenticity when western red cedar is readily available.

Early wood shingles were riven and then smoothed with a draw knife. Modern wood shingles are sawn and closely resemble the early shingles. Some people make the mistake of using hand-split cedar shakes on an antique house, thinking they are more authentic, but they look nothing like an early riven and smoothed shingle.

Wood shingles on the step roof and standing seam copper on the shallow pitch roof.

Modern shingles are eighteen inches long and assorted widths. They are called perfections, but the name is misleading, as they are prone to cupping and splitting and require regular maintenance. I have found that taper sawn shingles perform better and look more like an early roof shingle than

Wood shingles are high maintenance.

Taper-sawn shingles have thicker butts.

perfections. Taper sawn shingles are also eighteen inches long, but are thicker than perfections. The butt end of a taper sawn shingle is about one-half-inch thick while the butt of a perfection is more like three-eighths-inch thick. The additional thickness makes them far less susceptible to cupping and splitting. As you might expect, taper sawn shingles are a little pricier than perfections.

Wood shingles were nailed to rough-cut sheathing boards called roofers. Gaps were left between the roofers to allow air to circulate under the shingles. It is important to the longevity of a wood shingle roof that the shingles be allowed to dry from the underside after a rain.

Slate shingles were used in Boston and other urban areas where the spread of fire was an issue. They were also found on homes in western Vermont, near where slate was quarried. Slate shingles make an extremely durable roof that can easily last one hundred years. This longevity does not come cheap— slate is a very expensive roofing material. The main disadvantage is that they are heavy and require an extremely robust roof structure to hold them up. It would be unwise to put slate shingles on a roof that previously held wood shingles without reinforcing the structure first.

For low-pitch roofs, metal roofing is a wise choice. Early metal roofs were made of tin-coated steel. Tin is not a viable roofing material today, but standing-seam copper is a good alternative. Copper is expensive, but you will never have to replace it in your lifetime.

Gutters and Downspouts

Properly functioning gutters and downspouts will extend the life of exterior siding and keep cellars drier. However, poorly functioning gutters are worse than no gutters at all. On my own house, I must confess, the gutters have been more dysfunctional than functional, despite considerable effort and expense. The gutters are built into the cornice and lined with copper. The soldered joints in the copper lining frequently leak and water backs up under the shingles in the winter. I have had to rebuild sections of the cornice more than once when the gutter joints failed. Usually the only clue that the gutters are leaking is when rot appears on the underside of the cornice. Where the built-in gutters have proven impossible to maintain, I have extended the roof

Built-in gutters are part of the cornice.

Half-round copper gutter.

shingles over them and let the rainwater cascade to the ground. A wise man knows when to surrender.

External gutters are far more practical than built-in gutters. Modern aluminum ogee gutters look hopelessly wrong on an antique house, but half-round gutters look just right.

V-trough gutters are an alternative to metal gutters. They are easy to make out of two boards. The bottom of the trough can be sealed with caulk, but if you really don't want them to leak, it is smarter to line them with copper. They were common on early homes, but not surprisingly, few have survived.

V-trough gutter.

Clapboard Siding

Clapboards remain the most common siding material on New England homes. Early clapboards were riven and then shaved smooth with a draw knife. Since it was difficult to make a riven clapboard much more than four feet long, homes were sided with a lot of short pieces with lots of joints.

The joints were not simply square-cut and butted the way

Beaded clapboard and corner board.

Skived clapboard joints.

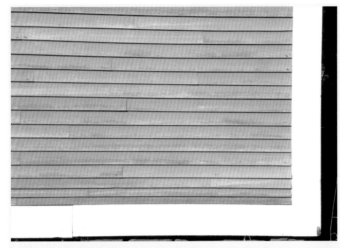
Graduated clapboards.

they are today. The ends of the clapboards were tapered with an adze and lapped two inches. A single rose-head nail would secure both clapboards. This type of joint is often called a scarf but the correct term is skived. A skived joint was more watertight than a butt joint and required half as many nails.

On first-period homes, the clapboards were nailed directly to the wall studs. By the early eighteenth century, it was becoming more common to have a layer of horizontal sheathing boards under the clapboards.

Sawn clapboards were first introduced in the 1820s. A water-powered up and down sawmill would cut narrow boards for clapboards. They were often of uniform thickness unlike a riven clapboard. The face of the clapboard would be hand-planed to remove the saw marks. Sometimes the clapboard would have a rabbet cut on the back of the bottom edge. The sawn boards tended to cup since they were mostly flat grain rather than vertical grain.

Circular sawmills were commonplace by 1830. A saw was developed that could radially cut tapered clapboards with all vertical grain. The face of the clapboard would still have to be hand-planed. These radially sawn clapboards were considerably more affordable than riven or water sawn clapboards. There are still a few mills in New England producing pine and spruce radially sawn clapboards by this method. One drawback of this method is that the clapboard length is limited to six feet.

The clapboard ends were tapered with an adz for a skived joint. *Courtesy of Jack Sobon.*

The spacing of the clapboards was sometimes graduated. The bottom course would have a two-and-a-half-inch exposure that would gradually increase to four-and-a-half inches. This gave superior weather resistance at the bottom of the wall where the siding tended to get wetter. There are many homes where the siding was only graduated on the front wall, suggesting that it was more fashion than function.

Today, vertical grain, western red cedar clapboards are readily available and affordable in long lengths. They last longer than pine with far fewer joints. They are not as historically authentic, but they are a practical alternative.

Fish scale shingles, Knapp Tavern, Greenwich, Connecticut.

There was no tradition of using shingles for siding in England and the idea did not occur to early New Englanders. The Dutch introduced shingle siding to America and the idea caught on. Dutch shingles were three feet long and often had curved butts that resembled fish scales. The curved butts were not just decorative, they actually shed water better than a square-cut butt, which is probably why fish have them.

Shingle siding was less costly than clapboard siding and was considered less formal. It is not uncommon to find an antique home with clapboards on the front and shingles on the sides and back wall. My own home has shingles that were tightly laid to resemble clapboards if you didn't look too close.

Faux stone—wood made to look like ashlar stone masonry. Col. William Lee house, Marblehead, Massachusetts.

Clapboards were sometimes only used on the front.

Chapter Twenty
FLOORS, WALLS, AND CEILINGS

Floors, walls, and ceilings are the inner skin of a home. They are the surfaces that define the inner space. Early first-period homes had crude inner skins with earthen floors, mud walls, and exposed timber ceilings. Rooms were small, ceilings were low, and spaces had all the charm of cave dwellings. A century later, fine homes had interior finishes that were nothing short of elegant, with wide-plank floors, raised panel walls, and plaster ceilings.

Wide-Plank Floors

White pine planks were the predominant flooring in New England homes. Pine was not necessarily the best choice for a floor. It is a soft wood that is easily marred. Oak is a much more durable material, and oak trees were more dominant in the New England forests. So why was white pine the floor of choice? It was one of those Yankee thrift things. Pine boards were far easier to mill than oak. A pine board could be sawn in half the time of an oak board and the saw blade would not need to be sharpened as often. Pine boards were also a lot easier to nail down than oak boards. Occasionally you will find a home with oak floors in the kitchen or keeping room and pine everywhere else. Oak was reserved for rooms that got a lot of use and abuse, but pine was still good enough for the fancy parlor.

Floor boards were random widths. The narrowest boards were reserved for the first floor and the widest boards were used in the attic. Widths up to twenty inches were common. While today people cherish the very wide boards, in the day they were considered a bit shabby. Narrow boards took longer to lay and required more nails in an age when nails were expensive.

The boards were face nailed with rose-head nails directly to the timber floor joists. The edges were sometimes left square, but more often they were shiplapped. On the first floor, they were usually laid over a subfloor to cut down on the cold, damp, cellar air rising through the joints. Everywhere else, the floor boards were laid directly on the floor joists.

The floor boards were left bare and never varnished. To

Wide-plank pine floors were left unfinished.

If you are considering finishing your pine floors with polyurethane, don't do it!

clean them, homeowners would scrub them with sand. In the finest homes, the pine floor boards would sometimes be painted. Occasionally a multi-color geometric design would be painted on the floor, with a contrasting border or maybe even diamond checkerboarding. But the floors were never varnished.

White pine is a pale white color when it is first sawn, which explains the name. When exposed to sunlight over time, it darkens to a deep honey color referred to as pumpkin pine. Some people believe that pumpkin pine is a species of tree, but in fact, it is eastern white pine with an aged patina.

Today, people expect wood floors to be sanded smooth and varnished with polyurethane. That is a great idea for hardwood floors but a really bad idea for pine floors. I have learned that lesson the hard way. Like everyone else, I sanded the floors in my house and varnished them with polyurethane. They looked great at first, but that did not last long.

Polyurethane forms a hard film or crust that does not penetrate below the surface. When soft pine is subjected to wear, the film flakes off. If you try recoating the surface, it will never blend in.

We have always had dogs. They are lovable companions, but they have not been kind to our pine floors, and a woman can be even worse. In the early 1980s, I had my office in my home. I had a secretary who was fond of wearing high heels to work. Every step she took left a small dimple in the floor. Craters appeared in the floor under her desk and in front of the copier. I have gotten into the habit of taking my shoes off in the house.

When all else failed, I painted the floors.

Floor sanding must be done with a light touch. Drum sanders designed for hardwood floors will excavate a trench in a pine floor if allowed to pause in one spot for more than a brief instant. I now only use a hand-held random orbit sander on my floors.

I have tried every modern floor finish on my floors—oil-based polyurethane, acrylic-based polyurethane, natural varnish, lacquer, and shellac. The only clear finish that really works on pine floors is a penetrating Tung oil. It usually takes about seven coats of Tung oil to build up a durable finish. If the floors became worn, you can add more coats and they will blend in nicely.

Out of desperation, I have painted the floors in high-traffic areas with alkyd-based porch paint. I consider it a strategic retreat, but it is actually more historically correct than a clear finish.

Walls of Wood

In the seventeenth century, lime for plaster was in short supply and iron nails to secure plaster lath were expensive. A more practical way of finishing interior walls was needed. Wood was plentiful and a natural choice. As you might have guessed, eastern white pine was the preferred wood species for building interior partition walls and finishing the inside of exterior walls.

Interior partition walls were built of one-inch-thick vertical boards that spanned from the floor to the ceiling. At first they were plain boards with shiplap edges and maybe a

Keeping room with paneled fireplace wall.

FEATHER EDGE PANELING

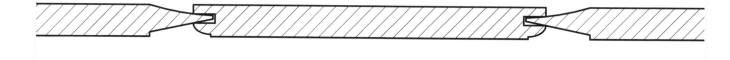

decorative bead, but they soon evolved into feather edge paneling. Alternate boards would have both edges grooved, or both edges feathered. This type of construction allowed the boards to expand and contract freely with changes in moisture content.

Exterior walls frequently had wood wainscoting. The window stools were extended across the walls to create a chair rail that capped the wainscot. Horizontal boards made up the

Feather edge boards.

wainscot. In the finer homes, raised panels set in a frame of stiles and rails replaced the horizontal wainscot boards. The raised panel wainscoting had such an elegant look that it remained popular throughout the Georgian period.

Raised paneling also became popular for the walls surrounding the fireplaces. These paneled "room ends" were finely crafted and sometimes capped with a dentilled cornice or flanked by carved cupboards. The paneled room end became a defining characteristic of high-style Georgian homes.

Raised panel wainscoting.

Plaster and Lath

Plaster walls and ceilings brought refinement to the interior of New England homes. As plaster became more affordable, timber framing was no longer left exposed as the ceiling. Less effort was expended on planing timbers smooth and summer beams were made shallower so they would not project below the plaster surface. When they did, they were cased with finish boards.

Plaster was a three-coat operation—a scratch coat, a brown coat, and a white coat. The plaster was made from lime putty and sand with animal hair sometimes added. It was applied to a wood lath substrate. Prior to 1825, lath was made from strips of riven oak, or thin sawn boards that were split and stretched apart called accordion lath. After 1825, sawn lath became the norm.

Plaster on wood lath.

Accordion lath split from a thin board. Courtesy of Historic Deerfield.

The lath was nailed to the wall studs or ceiling joists with gaps left between the slats. The lath would be soaked with water before the scratch coat was applied so that the wood would not suck water out of the plaster. The plaster did not actually stick to the wood lath. The snots of plaster that oozed through the gaps would form "keys" that anchored the plaster in place. If the keys break off, as often happens with older plaster, the plaster will separate from the lath. If that happens, you will need to replace the plaster or anchor it back to the lath.

One method of anchoring failed plaster is to use plaster washers. Plaster washers are about the size of a quarter. Drywall screws are used to attach the washers to the lath. If the plaster does not crumble and self-destruct when the washers are installed, the surface is skim coated with joint compound to hide the washers and screws.

Another method of anchoring failed plaster uses a plaster adhesive that comes in a caulking tube. A series of holes are drilled through the plaster and the adhesive is injected into the holes. Temporary plastic disc washers are screwed into the lath to hold the plaster until the adhesive sets.

Plaster washers and plaster adhesives are often effective for repairing small areas of failed plaster. If the problem area is more extensive, replacement is a smarter option.

In modern construction, drywall, commonly referred to as sheetrock, is typically used in place of plaster. Sheetrock has many fine qualities. It can be installed quickly and inexpensively. It does not take a lot of skill, and a do-it-yourselfer can quickly master the technique of taping the joints. Despite these fine qualities, I have never been able to really warm up to it. Call me old-fashioned, I just like the look and feel of real plaster.

Today's pre-mixed plaster is made of gypsum rather than lime. Gypsum sets quicker and harder than lime plaster. Perlite is used instead of sand for the aggregate. Gypsum lath, called blueboard, is used instead of wood lath. Blueboard looks a lot like sheetrock except it has a blue paper face that plaster sticks to. Only a single, thin coat of plaster is needed over blueboard rather than the traditional three-coat process.

When I use new plaster in an antique home, I prefer a rustic textured finish. Instead of a smooth white coat mix, I use a base coat mix that is really intended to be used for a scratch or brown coat. Paint pigment can be mixed with the plaster to produce an integral color that does not require painting.

This plaster ceiling has separated from the lath.

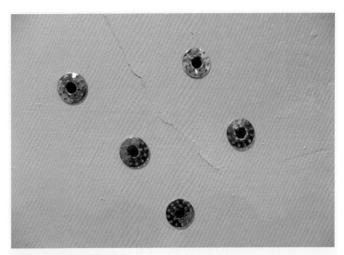
Plaster washers.

Master plasterer Mike Zordan plasters the ceiling between timber rafters.

Rustic textured plaster with integral color.

Ceiling Treatments

Antique homes typically have low ceilings by modern standards. Often the ceilings are less than eight feet high. Low ceilings can make a space feel cozy, but they can also feel a little claustrophobic.

Exposed beam ceilings have long been fashionable and make a space feel taller. Unless your house was built in the seventeenth century, the timber beams were never intended to be exposed.

When I first purchased my home, the upstairs bath had been leaking for years. Consequently the plaster ceiling below the bath was partially collapsed. I decided to take the whole living room ceiling down and expose the timbers. I

Living room with exposed timber ceiling. *Suzanne Sheridan Photography.*

knew at the time that it was not historically accurate to have an exposed beam ceiling, but I did it anyway.

I cleaned the accumulated dirt and grunge off the timbers with a mild abrasive blast referred to as corn blasting. It is like sandblasting except it uses ground-up corn cob for an abrasive rather than sand. Despite my best efforts to seal the room off with plastic, a cloud of dust and debris went everywhere, but the beams came out looking great with a honey-color patina. I finished the ceiling with plaster between the beams. The exposed-beam ceiling adds visual interest to the room and I like the look.

Cathedral ceilings have also been popular for several decades. They were not a feature of antique homes. In 1982,

Cathedral ceiling for my office, circa 1982.

Great room with elliptical vaulted ceiling.

I renovated a second-floor wing of the house that had been added circa 1890. It had no redeeming architectural features on the inside, so I felt at liberty to gut the space. I put in a cathedral ceiling and converted the space into an office for my business. At the time, I really liked the look.

A couple of decades later, long after I moved my office out of the house, my tastes had matured and I no longer felt that the 1980s look was appropriate in an antique house. So I gutted the space again and gave it more of a period look. I built cabinets, window seats, and bookcases for the room. I created an elliptical, vaulted plaster ceiling inspired by a tavern ballroom I had seen in Deerfield, Massachusetts.

Barnard Tavern ballroom. *Courtesy of Historic Deerfield.*

The King's Broad Arrow, 1691–1775

Following the defeat of the Spanish Armada in 1588, the British Royal Navy ruled the seas. Being an island nation, it was crucial to England's national security that they maintain naval superiority over their adversaries, and naval shipbuilding became a strategic priority.

The forests in England had an ample supply of oaks for building the ship hulls but no tall conifers suitable for ship masts and spars. The Royal Navy was forced to purchase mast timbers from the Baltic fir forests of what is today Northern Poland. The imported Baltic firs were expensive and their supply could easily be cut off in time of war by an enemy blockading the straits between Denmark and Sweden. It eventually occurred to the Admiralty that there was an abundant supply of tall white pine and spruce trees growing in their New England colonies that could be free for the taking.

Parliament set about passing a series of acts to secure the New England supply of mast timber. These enabling acts came to be known as the king's Broad Arrow policy. Mast agents surveyed the forests and marked suitable mast trees with the king's Broad Arrow blaze. The blaze was made with three axe strokes that formed an upward pointing arrow.

White pines and spruce trees grew predominantly in Maine, coastal New Hampshire, and northern Massachusetts, so that is where the king's mast agents went to work. They only surveyed forests within ten miles of a navigable waterway and only marked trees greater than twenty-four inches in diameter.

Ship masts and spars.

King's Broad Arrow blaze on a pine tree.

Eventually, Portsmouth, New Hampshire, became the epicenter of the mast trade.

Any colonist caught in the act of cutting down a tree marked with the Broad Arrow could be severely fined. There was one exception to the rule—if a tree blew down in a windstorm, you were allowed to harvest the timber and yield a "windfall profit." New Englanders flaunted the law and got in the habit of making their own wind.

New Englanders cared little for the needs of the Royal Navy and preferred to harvest white pines for making floor boards. To avoid prosecution from the king's mast agents, the colonists typically made the floor boards narrower than twenty-four inches.

Chapter Twenty-One
WINDOWS AND DOORS

Windows are the eyes of a home. They not only let daylight in, but also bring a view of the outside in, connecting a home with its site. On the exterior, it is the windows that make a house sparkle.

Sadly, antique windows are under-appreciated and often mistreated. Renovators are quick to discard rather than restore old windows. Modern replacement windows hardly ever look right on an antique home and seldom live up to the performance claims made by window salesmen. An antique home with vinyl-clad replacement windows is like Paul Newman with brown eyes.

Glass

Window glass was an expensive commodity and in short supply in early New England. Only the finest homes could afford to have lots of windows. Glass was imported from England until after the revolution.

The first successful glassworks in the colonies was built in 1739 by Caspar Wistar in Allotar, New Jersey. Wistar's glass was used in Philadelphia homes, but not much of it found its way to New England. Roads were poor and it was more costly to transport glass from New Jersey than to ship it from England. In 1792, the Boston Crown Glass Manufactory began producing window glass for the New England market.

Antique window with mouth-blown glass.

Glass-making exhibit at the Corning Museum of Glass. Crown glass-making is shown on the left and cylinder glass-making is on the right. *Courtesy of Kenin Bassart of The Constant Rambler.*

All window glass was mouth-blown prior to 1900. Mouth-blown glass is not perfectly flat; it is a little wavy and contains bubbles and other imperfections. At the time, these imperfections were considered defects, but today they are considered charming.

Two methods were used for manufacturing mouth-blown glass—the crown glass method and the cylinder glass method. To produce crown glass, a lump of molten glass would be spun to form a large disc about four feet in diameter. The very center of the disc, called the bull's eye, was considered unusable for window glass. The old Yankees would use the bull's eyes for transom windows over doorways rather than discard it. Crown glass often has a slight purple tint, uneven thickness, and concentric circular striations.

Cylinder glass was made by blowing a huge bottle. The ends of the bottle would be cut off while the glass was still hot. The remaining cylinder would then be slit lengthwise and flattened out in an oven. Cylinder glass became popular after 1825. It was cheaper to produce than crown glass and yielded fewer imperfections and larger sizes. It is rare to find crown glass in an older window since it was common practice in the nineteenth century to replace the crown glass with cylinder glass.

Bull's eye glass transom.

Restoration glass available today is usually made by the cylinder glass method. When I replace cracked or broken window lites, I often use restoration glass. A window sash with a mix of new glass and mouth-blown glass has a nice antique look. If all of the window lites are mouth-blown glass, the distortion of the view through the window can be annoying—you need some modern glass mixed in.

First-Period Casement Windows

In the seventeenth century, window glass was expensive and hard to come by. Modest homes used oiled paper instead of glass in their windows. The crown glass that was available only came in small, diamond-shaped lites called quarrels.

This first-period house had no windows on the back.

Casement window with diamond-shaped quarrels set in lead cames.

Windows were either fixed or casement style with iron hinges. The quarrels were set in lead cames and anchored to iron bars.

Windows were small and few. It was not unusual to have no windows at all on the rear wall. Inside, the space was dark and gloomy.

There are few, if any, surviving examples of original first-period casement windows. Those on museum homes are mostly reproductions. When single-hung windows became popular in the eighteenth century, owners of older homes were quick to replace their old and tired casements windows.

Single-Hung and Double-Hung Windows

The Georgian era saw a major advance in window technology—the development of the operable sash window. Eighteenth-century operable sash windows were mostly single hung, with the top sash fixed and only the bottom sash operable. Nineteenth century windows were typically double hung, with both the upper and lower sash operable. The

9/9 single-hung window with a pediment crown.

Variety of window sizes made with 7×9-inch lites.

Different size windows, both with 12/12 pattern—this is just plain wrong!

SINGLE-HUNG 12/12 WINDOW ANATOMY

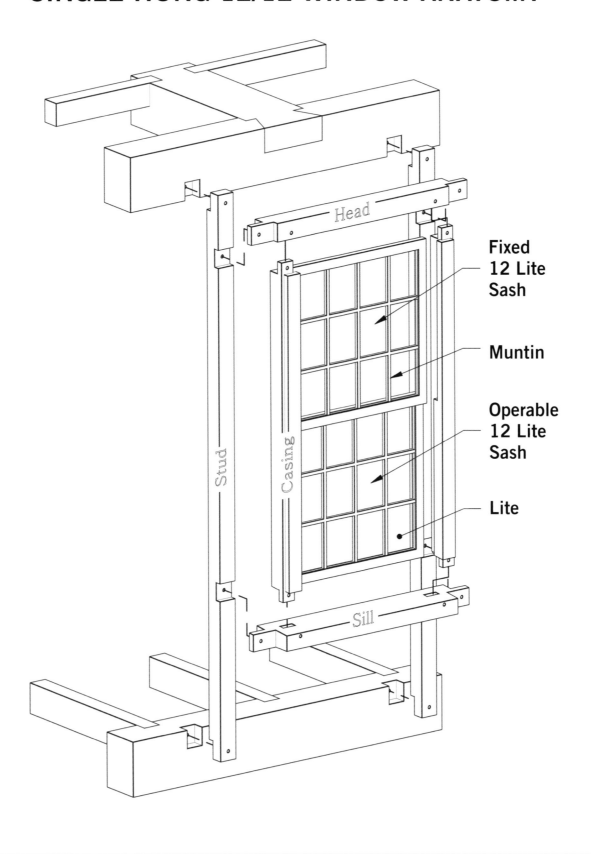

Head

Fixed 12 Lite Sash

Muntin

Operable 12 Lite Sash

Lite

Stud

Casing

Sill

MUNTIN PROFILE

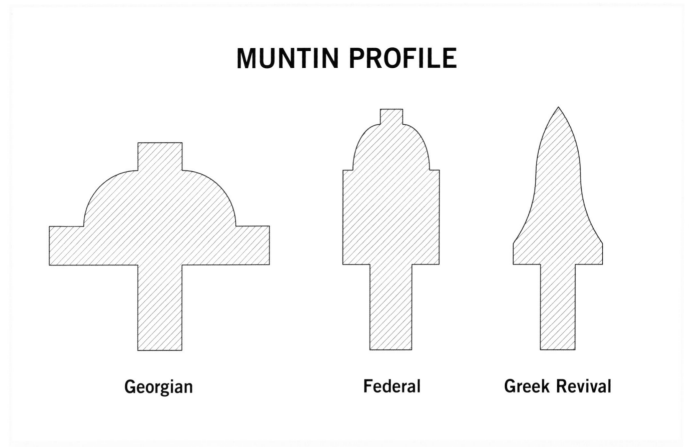

Georgian   **Federal**   **Greek Revival**

Muntin profiles through the ages.

double-hung window is still the most popular style of window.

Sash windows were made possible by the availability of rectangular panes of crown glass. The individual window panes were called lites. Windows are described by the number of lites in each sash. For instance, a window with twelve lites in the upper sash and eight lites in the lower sash is called a twelve over eight (12/8) window. Common window configurations were 12/12, 12/8, 9/9, 9/6, and 6/6.

Imported crown glass came precut to one size only. Prior to 1750, lites measured six by eight inches. From 1750 to 1825, lites measured seven by nine inches. From 1825 to 1850, cylinder glass lites measured eight by ten inches. After 1850, much larger pieces of cylinder glass became available.

All the windows on a house would have been made of the same size lites. For instance, a Georgian period house would have all seven by nine lites. Different window sizes would be achieved by varying the number of lites in the sash. For instance, the large windows would be 12/12 and the small windows 6/6, but the individual lite sizes would all be the same. The biggest mistake that renovators and architects make with replacement windows is not maintaining consistent lite sizes.

Palladians, Lunettes, and Other Fancy Stuff

The finest homes were accented with signature windows to delight the eye. They brought light into attics and entry halls and were seldom operable. Signature windows were an opportunity for the joiner to display his skill and artistry. Particular window motifs were often found only within a very local region and were the signature of an individual craftsman and his apprentices.

A lunette window.

Oval spider web window.

A Palladian window above the entry.

Shutters

Window shutters were intended to protect the windows from the elements and reduce drafts, not for decoration. During the Georgian period, interior shutters were found on the finest homes. The shutters slid into pockets or folded up accordion style.

Exterior shutters did not become commonplace until the federal period. Shutters with louvers were called blinds. In the summer, blinds let fresh air in while keeping out the sun, bugs, and birds.

Pocket shutters.

Accordion shutters.

Exterior shutters should be mounted on hinges and sized to fit the window.

Restore or Replace?

This is a difficult and important decision. Do you rip out the old windows or fix them? I'll make it easy for you. If your house has the original window sashes, fix them. If the sashes are replacements, tear them out and put in good reproduction windows. In my opinion, it is an act of vandalism to trash original antique windows.

It is usually easy to determine if the sashes are original to the house. Older sashes usually have mortises in the mullions where the muntin bars are tenoned to them. Some of the window lites will be wavy crown or cylinder glass, and the muntin bar profile and lite size will be consistent with the period of the house.

Depending on the condition of the windows, restoration may be as simple as repairing dried out glazing putty and repainting. If the sashes are in poor condition, restoration may also involve removing the glass, stripping the paint, and epoxy repair of rotted sections. Adding weather-stripping is always a good idea, and if there are no sash weights, spring balances can be added.

Restoring antique window sash.

Mullion has a mortise to accept the muntin tenon.

Storm windows are a necessity.

Reproduction true divided lite window with insulated glass and pocket shutters on the inside.

Restored windows with storm windows will usually have comparable if not better energy performance than a new double-glazed window. Storm windows not only increase the thermal R-value of a window, but more importantly, they significantly decrease air infiltration. Storm windows are typically installed on the outside of the windows, but there are also systems made to be installed on the inside. The advantage of an exterior storm is that it protects the window sash from the weather. The disadvantage is that the windows don't look as good from the outside. The advantage of interior storms is that the windows look great from the outside. The disadvantage is the windows don't look so good from the inside. When you weigh it all out, I think exterior storm windows make more sense.

In an attempt to be authentic, some people will have custom wood storm windows made for their antique house, not realizing that wood storm windows are an early twentieth–century thing. Wood storms obscure the windows and are out of place on an early period home.

If the windows must be replaced, avoid factory-made windows. They hardly ever look right on an antique house. Factory-made windows are usually vinyl or aluminum clad with simulated divided lites (SDL), which means that there is one big piece of glass with a grill glued to the glass that vaguely resembles muntin bars. It is rare for a factory replacement window to have the appropriate lite size and configuration. A reproduction window is usually a smarter choice. A historic millwork shop can produce a proper reproduction wood window with true divided lites made of insulated, double-glazed glass. I like to make some of the lites with restoration glass randomly placed in the sash to simulate the look of an antique window. The reproduction window will look just like the original windows, but with proper weather-stripping and concealed spring balances. A reproduction window does not necessarily cost more than a good-quality factory-made window.

Doors and Doorways

Early doors were crude batten doors made from vertical planks nailed to horizontal battens or horizontal planks. They were not fancy, but they were easy to build and did their job of keeping out the weather and intruders.

Frame and panel doors became commonplace by the early eighteenth century. They were more permanent than batten doors and did not warp as easily. Frame and panel doors could not be slapped together by a carpenter; they required a skilled joiner to make. This type of door construction is still in use today, although modern frame and panel doors are a bit thicker than period doors.

The front door was often framed by a decorative doorway called a frontispiece. Without a distinctive frontispiece, all homes would have looked alike. The most celebrated fron-

tispieces are Connecticut Valley doorways found in the river towns that stretched from Wethersfield, Connecticut, up river to Deerfield, Massachusetts. They are characterized by a pair of narrow doors framed by carved pilasters and a pediment. The narrow doors are a bit clumsy to walk through, but they were necessitated by the narrow passage between the door and stair in center chimney homes.

Georgian period frontispieces were typically flush with the exterior wall, offering little protection from the weather. This design flaw was corrected on federal and Greek revival homes with porch roofs supported by classical columns. Federal frontispieces also sported sidelights flanking the door and ornate transom windows that brought daylight into the entry.

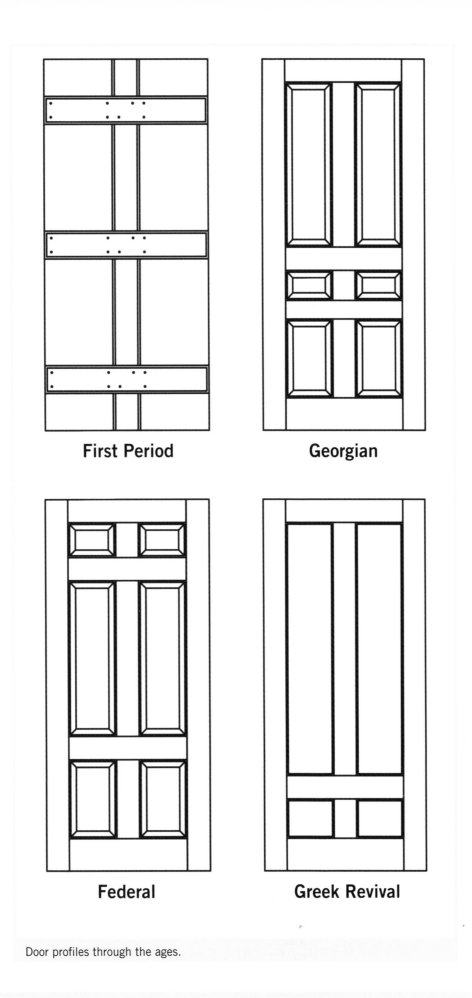

First Period　　　**Georgian**

Federal　　　**Greek Revival**

Door profiles through the ages.

Batten door. *Courtesy of Maurer & Shepherd.*

Frame and panel door.

Connecticut Valley doorway with a broken scroll pediment.

Transom windows over interior doors are commonly found in Nantucket homes.

Chapter Twenty-One: Windows and Doors | **Part Three**

Chapter Twenty-Two
HEAVY METAL—IRON HARDWARE

Under a spreading chestnut tree the village smithy stands; the smith, a mighty man is he, with large and sinewy hands, and the muscles of his brawny arms are strong as iron bands.

—Henry Wadsworth Longfellow

Iron hardware is the jewelry that adorns an antique house. When applied tastefully, it adds beauty to the architecture, but if applied with a heavy hand, it can be garish.

Iron Plantations

In the early years, most of the iron products consumed in New England were imported from Old England. But imported iron was becoming increasingly costly. English forests were vanishing at an alarming rate as hardwoods were harvested for the production of charcoal to feed the iron blast furnaces. As trees became scarce, the cost of charcoal climbed, driving up the cost of iron production.

In America, the hardwood forests were vast. The temptation to build iron plantations in the new world was irresistible to the English ironmasters. The first American iron enterprise was built in 1619 at Falling Creek, Virginia, near Jamestown. Its success was short-lived. In 1622 a Native American raid destroyed the ironworks, and all of the ironworkers were put to the hatchet. Virginians gave up on iron and put their energies into the more lucrative crop of tobacco.

Saugus Ironworks.

In New England, iron production was more successful. In 1650 an ironworks was built at Saugus, Massachusetts. They mined bog ore, or limonite, from the marshes and smelted it into pig iron at the blast furnace.

Beckley blast furnace, East Canaan, Connecticut.

Pig iron contained a high percentage of carbon, which made it brittle. Molten pig iron could be poured into sand molds to cast useful items such as pots and kettles, but it could not be shaped by smiths without shattering.

Pig iron was converted to wrought iron by being reheated in a finery forge, which removed most of the carbon. The refined iron was then hammered into bars of wrought iron for sale to blacksmiths who would turn it into tools, implements, and hardware. Iron bars were also rolled and slit into rods for nail manufacturing.

Within a few decades, ironworks were being built throughout New England. There are a few essential ingredients needed for iron production. Iron ore is an obvious ingredient. Since iron is one of the most plentiful elements on the surface of the Earth, and makes up most of Earth's core, suitable ore is not hard to find.

Charcoal was needed to fuel the blast furnaces. To make charcoal, cordwood was stacked in large mounds and covered with leaves and earth. The mound would be ignited and the fire starved of oxygen. The smoldering fire would burn off the volatile compounds in the wood, leaving behind a pile of charcoal that was almost pure carbon. The charcoal from more than two acres of hardwood forest was needed to fuel a blast furnace for a single day. It did not take long to turn a dense forest into an open, scarred landscape. Charcoal production was the job of grubby, forest-dwelling characters called colliers who were always covered in soot, smelled bad, and were avoided by everybody else.

Limestone was needed as a flux. Iron ore, charcoal, and limestone were continuously fed into the blast furnace, which burned night and day. As the ore melted, the limestone would combine with the impurities and float to the top as a slag, while molten iron sank to the bottom of the furnace, where it collected in a crucible that would be periodically tapped.

While iron ore and hardwood forests were plentiful in New England, suitable limestone deposits were harder to come by. Oyster shells could be used in a pinch, but vast quantities were needed.

Water power was needed to power the bellows that generated the blast of air needed for the furnaces and to operate the trip hammers that forged pig iron into wrought iron.

The Housatonic River Valley of Northwest Connecticut was ideally suited for iron production. The river runs parallel to a geological marble formation of metamorphosed limestone known as the Stockbridge formation. The Stockbridge marble formation continues north through Massachusetts and into Vermont.

The region was densely wooded with mature oak forests ideal for charcoal production and, by a stroke of fate, a seam of rich limonite ore was found to run alongside the marble formation. It was an ironmaster's dream come true.

The early ironworks in the region were small, water-powered, bloomer forges, but it was not long before full-scale iron plantations were being built with blast furnaces and finery forges.

Salisbury, Connecticut, soon became the rust belt of New England—long before anybody thought of producing iron in places like Pittsburgh, Bethlehem, Gary, or Baltimore.

New England iron production became so successful that iron producers back in England began complaining that the colonies were cutting into their profits. In 1750 the English iron producers were successful at lobbying Parliament to ban the construction of any new ironworks producing wrought iron in the colonies. Naturally, New Englanders ignored the ban.

During the American Revolution, Connecticut ironworks were producing cannon and munitions for the Continental Army. Many of them continued to operate until the end of World War I when they could no longer compete with the mills in Pennsylvania that were producing Bessemer steel and using coke as a fuel instead of charcoal. Coke was made by roasting coal—at the time, coke was not a soft drink or illegal substance.

Iron plantations were both capital and labor intensive. Labor would prove to be tougher to come by than the necessary raw materials in a region full of opportunities for industrious individuals. Plantations employed upwards of one hundred workers, including furnace workers, founders, blacksmiths, miners, wood cutters, colliers, and teamsters. An iron plantation typically included a stylish home for the ironmaster and scores of less elegant quarters for everybody else. The plantation model persisted in the iron industry until the end of the nineteenth century. When the massive Sparrows Point integrated steel mill was built in Baltimore in 1891, it included homes, shops, and schools for 2,500 mill workers and their families. It was a complete community and the last of the iron plantations.

The New England iron industry was the beginning of America's industrial revolution. It predated the railroads and textile mills by more than a century and was the start of the transition from an agrarian to an urban society in New England.

The popular image of a blacksmith is a big, burly guy, with bulging biceps, shoeing horses under a spreading chestnut tree. Actually, none of that is really true.

Blacksmiths did not shoe horses—that was the job of the farrier. Farriers did use anvils and coal forges to heat the shoes, but that is where the similarity ends. Being a farrier is more about shaping a horse's hoof than shaping iron shoes.

The blacksmith made tools, plow blades, andirons, chains, wagon wheel tires, nails, and hardware—virtually anything made of iron. He also repaired them when they broke or wore out. Every town needed a blacksmith. You could get by without a minister, but not without a blacksmith.

A blacksmith worked inside a dimly lit shop called a smithy. It was important to be able to accurately discern the color of the hot iron, and that could not be done in bright light. In the center of the smithy was the brick forge where wrought iron was heated to forging temperature in a charcoal or soft coal fire with the aid of a bellows. A few feet away from the forge stood an anvil mounted on a section of tree trunk buried in the earth. The smithy was a dingy, cluttered, soot-covered shop filled

Blacksmith shop, Eastfield Village.

with a variety of specialty tools—hardies, fullers, swages, mandrels, punches, and tongs. Despite all the fancy tools, the majority of work was done with just a cross-peen hammer and the anvil.

Iron is a stubborn material to shape at room temperature, but once heated in a forge, it is transformed into a malleable material that can be shaped with well-directed blows of a hammer. Wrought iron was forged at an orange or yellow heat by a few basic operations. "Drawing out" involved stretching and thinning the iron. "Upsetting" was the process

of fattening the iron to create a bulge. Holes were made by punching and were then enlarged or elongated with a drift.

Forge welding is the most dramatic process of the blacksmith's craft. The pieces to be welded are coated with a borax flux and heated in the forge to a bright yellow to white heat. The iron pieces are hammered together amidst a shower of sparks as the flux is squeezed out of the weld.

The blacksmith was not a big guy—he was typically of average size and build. He was certainly in good shape with toned biceps but his work did not require brute strength—it required rapid, deliberate, precisely placed strikes of the hammer. He often had an assistant called a striker who was a big guy. To be a striker, brawn was more important than finesse. The striker would stand on the opposite side of the anvil and strike the hot iron with a sledge hammer in the exact spot where the blacksmith had just struck it. It was a well-choreographed operation.

Some blacksmiths were also whitesmiths. While a blacksmith shapes hot iron, a whitesmith shapes it cold by filing. Door locks and instruments are the work of the whitesmith.

The industrial revolution was not kind to the village blacksmith. By the second half of the nineteenth century, factories were mass producing iron products and the blacksmith's business went into a decline. In 1908 Henry Ford unveiled his Model T and needed skilled metalworkers to build them. He offered attractive salaries to any blacksmith who would come to Detroit and build cars. It was not a tough choice—many packed their bags and turned the shop over to the striker, which explains why old-timers remember blacksmiths as being burly guys.

The art of blacksmithing would have been lost forever had it not been for a new generation of artist blacksmiths who rediscovered the craft in the 1970s. Today it is not hard to find a skilled blacksmith capable of making perfect reproductions of iron hardware and iron artwork. Determined to master the craft myself, I built a forge in my barn thirty years ago and took some workshops at a local craft school. Although I am still not very good at it, I have mastered the basics and

Iron heated to a yellow glow is shaped on the anvil. *Courtesy of Bob Valentine.*

can repair or replace missing parts of old iron hardware that I scrounge up at flea markets. I can say from personal experience that blacksmithing is not nearly as easy as it looks.

Iron Nails

Nails were a critical and expensive component of early homes. Today we don't give a lot of thought or respect to nails. They are a mass-produced commodity that can be purchased for pennies, but that was not always the case. Prior to the industrial revolution, they were made by hand—one at a time, by blacksmiths and nail makers.

Timber frames may have been held together with wooden pegs called treenails, but everything else was secured with iron nails—floorboards, siding, roof shingles, plaster lath, and millwork. Even a modest size home required thousands of iron nails and each one had to be made by hand—one at a time.

Handmade iron nails.

A door fashionably adorned with rose-head nails.

Making iron nails was not hard and did not really demand the skill of a master blacksmith. Apprentices would start out making nails before moving on to more challenging tasks. Farmers could get into the nail-making business with a small coal forge, a crude anvil, and a few basic tools. In the southern colonies, slaves were put to work making nails.

Nails were forged from wrought iron nail rod made in a slitting mill like the one at the Saugus ironworks. Over one quarter of the iron produced at the time went into nail rod. A nail rod was a long, square bar about a quarter-inch wide and three feet long. One end of the nail rod would be heated in the forge and then hammered to a tapered point on the anvil. A notch would be made in the rod a couple of inches from the point with a chisel called a hardy mounted on the top of the anvil. The pointed end of the rod was inserted into a tool called a header and the rod was broken off at the notch. The head would be formed by hammering the butt end of the rod sticking out of the header. The hand forged head was called a rose-head. Then it was back in the fire with the nail rod to do it all over again. A blacksmith who was in a groove could produce a nail a minute.

Batten doors were held together with rose-head doornails that were clenched. The nails would be driven through the door and the point bent over so that it made a U-turn with the point driven back into the door. Clenching a nail was referred to as deadening—thus the expression "dead as a doornail." It became fashionable on the finer homes of the seventeenth century to pepper the face of the front door with rose-head nails in a diamond pattern. This was a garish display of wealth—showing off that you could waste expensive nails on decoration.

Like beer, nails were sold by the keg.

In the eighteenth century, England standardized the price of nails to protect the consumer from price gouging. The set price was a function of nail size; for instance, a two-and-a-half-inch nail sold for eight cents for one hundred nails. They became known as eight-penny nails and the name stuck. Today the penny weight nail designation is still in use.

Hand-forged rose-head nails.

Cut nails.

I have read stories of people in colonial times burning down their old house and sifting through the ashes to salvage the nails. I have not found any reliable documentary evidence that such a practice ever existed and I am dubious. The old Yankees were certainly thrifty and it was commonplace for them to repurpose an older house as an ell on the back of a newer home or as a woodshed, but is unlikely that they could bring themselves to intentionally burn it down. Of course, if a house or barn managed to burn down on its own, I don't doubt that they would have made an effort to salvage any nails they could find in the remains.

Sooner or later, somebody had to come up with a better way to produce iron nails. In 1795 Jacob Perkins patented a machine for making nails. He built a mill on the Powwow River in Amesbury, Massachusetts, to manufacture cut nails. The nails were sheared from an iron plate. The heads were still forged by hand and looked indistinguishable from the rose-heads on handmade nails. Eventually a machine was developed that could form the nail heads.

When Jacob Perkins' mill began producing cut nails in 1797, the price of nails became much more affordable. After that, there wasn't much call for handmade nails.

It is easy to distinguish a handmade nail from an early cut nail by examining the shank. A handmade nail has a shank

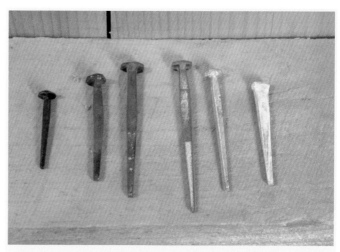
Reproduction nails by Tremont.

that tapers on all four sides, while a cut nail has a shank that tapers on only two sides.

When dating an antique home, the type of nails used provides a clue. If the house contains cut nails, it had to have been built after 1797. If the cut nails have a machine formed head, then the house was built after 1817.

Machine-made rose-head cut nails are available today from the Tremont Nail Company in Wareham, Massachusetts. They don't look exactly like an authentic old nail, but they are close enough for restoration work.

Iron Hardware

The local village blacksmith made, among other things, fancy door latches, strap hinges, and nails. Locks, bean latches, spring latches, and hinges were imported from England, even after the revolution. Specialty blacksmith shops in the Staffordshire area mass produced building hardware and the village blacksmith could not compete.

The Suffolk latch was the most common door latch used until 1800. The handle and cusps were forged from a single piece of iron. The cusp of the Suffolk latch came in a variety of decorative shapes—a bean, a spade, and an arrowhead.

The Norfolk latch became popular after 1800. It had a flat back plate and a D-shaped handle. The handles were sometimes decorated with a pewter ferrule. Norfolk latches were mass produced in specialty shops.

Both Suffolk latches and Norfolk latches had similar latch bar assemblies on the opposite side of the door.

Spring latches were a little more elegant and featured brass door knobs. They were imported from England and came in a square shape or a keyhole model.

Rim locks were used on exterior doors. They also featured brass door knobs and had a deadbolt lock that was operated with a key. The brass door knob was sometimes egg-shaped rather than round. Rim locks were the work of the whitesmith and included both cast and forged parts. They were commonly painted with a Japan black finish.

HL hinges were used on interior doors prior to the revolution. They were secured with clenched nails that were driven through square leather washers. It is rare to find leather washers intact since they have proven less durable than the iron. The hinges were painted the same color as the door—the idea of accenting iron hardware with black paint was a colonial revival thing.

H hinges and butterfly hinges were commonly used on cabinet doors.

Strap hinges were used on heavy exterior doors and on barn doors. Strap hinges were made by the local village blacksmith. The ends of the strap had a bean or spade profile to match the Suffolk latch cusp.

Cast iron butt hinges were first manufactured in 1775 and were an overnight sensation. They were imported from England both during and after the revolution. Unlike modern hinges, the pin was not removable.

Butt hinges were held in place with handmade screws that had a blunt end. Machine-made screws with a gimlet point were not introduced until 1846.

Besides door locks, whitesmiths also made kitchen appliances. The spit jack was the ultimate kitchen appliance of its day. It mounted above the great fireplace and had a clockwork mechanisim that turned a spit to roast meats, rotissere style.

Suffolk bean latch.

Suffolk spade latch.

Suffolk arrowhead latch.

Latch bar assembly.

Square spring latch.

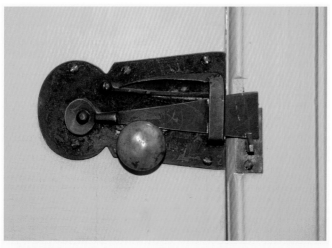

Keyhole spring latch.

Rim lock reproduction by D. C. Mitchell.

Inner workings of a rim lock.

HL hinge.

Butterfly hinge.

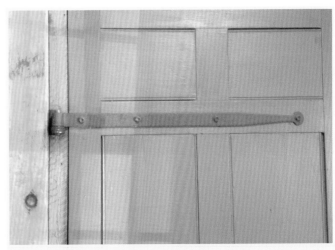

Strap hinge.

Cast iron butt hinge.

Pointless screws.

Norfolk latch.

H hinge.

Spit jack, Eastfield Village.

Strap hinges in a variety of shapes and sizes.

Master Blacksmith—Bob Valentine

Bob Valentine has been blacksmithing for forty years. His reproduction iron hardware is museum quality. The only difference between Bob's hardware and the antique originals is the lack of rust. He prides himself on "copying the signature of period blacksmiths." When not working at his Village Blacksmith Shop, he can be found at the Goshen Town Hall where he is the First Selectman.

These fancy Suffolk latches with decorative cusps were made by Bob Valentine. The originals were each found within a particular region of New England, which suggests they were made by a local blacksmith and not imported from England. Courtesy of Bob Valentine.

Bob at his forge on a snowy winter day. *Courtesy of Bob Valentine.*

Chapter Twenty-Three
KITCHENS AND BATHS

Historically correct bathroom.

Doing the dishes, Eastfield Village.

Kitchens and bathrooms are the most important rooms in a home. They are very personal spaces where we spend our special, quality time. They are also the most expensive rooms in a house. Kitchens and baths are particularly challenging spaces in an antique home because there is no historical precedent to follow.

Antique homes did not have kitchens and bathrooms in the modern sense. There certainly was a privy out back and a creek for bathing in when the mood struck. But most people today have been spoiled by indoor plumbing. While it is fun to reminisce about simpler times, we don't want to go back to them.

Meals were prepared in the great fireplace and the dishes were washed in a tub, or maybe a stone sink.

Hearth cooking can be fun on occasion. A turkey roasted on an open fire with a pumpkin pie baked in a beehive oven can make for a memorable Thanksgiving feast. But you are going to want to put the leftovers in the fridge and nuke them the next day in the microwave. The antique house experience does not have to include doing without modern conveniences and indoor plumbing.

So how do you make modern kitchens and baths fit in when they never really existed before? The trick is to borrow period-appropriate design elements from the rest of the house. There were no kitchen cabinets 200 years ago, but you can build cabinets that resemble cupboards and furniture from the period.

You can have modern appliances in the kitchen as long as they are not in your face. A refrigerator can be made to look like a pantry with paneled wood faces on the doors. Dishwashers can also have paneled wood faces and microwaves can tuck into cabinets.

Granite countertops, although popular, often look too modern. Soapstone is nice but requires frequent maintenance. My preferred countertop material is honed slate. It does not stain and is practically indestructible.

The same rules apply for bathrooms. Claw-foot tubs and Victorian plumbing fixtures look silly in a home that was built a century before the Victorian period. It is okay to use modern fixtures as long as they are not in your face. Avoid anything made of polished chrome.

Kitchen cabinets styled after period furniture.

The stove fits in.

Honed slate farm sink and countertops.

Hearth cooking with the stove and ovens built into the center chimney.

No need for an eat-in kitchen when the dining room is just a few steps away.

The refrigerator could be mistaken for a pantry.

A salvaged tin sink set in period cabinets.

Red slate countertop, copper sink, wood wainscot, and modern fixtures that blend in.

Wood wainscot beats ceramic tile.

Green limestone shower and no need for shower doors.

Chapter Twenty-Four
CABINETS AND MILLWORK

It is the woodwork that makes living in an antique home special—the paneled walls and wainscots, carved fireplace mantels, cornices, and cupboards. Without them, it would be like living in a sheetrocked postwar colonial.

The Joiner

Millwork, doors, window sashes, trim, and cabinets were the work of the joiner. The joiner was part carpenter and part cabinetmaker. He worked inside a shop and he worked with planes—lots of them. There were smoothing planes to flatten boards, jointer planes to straighten edges, plow planes to form grooves, and scores of molding planes to create every conceivable molding profile.

Joiner's shop at Eastfield Village—you can never have too many molding planes.

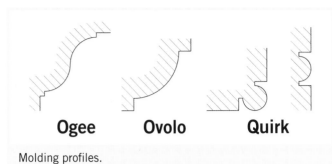

Ogee   **Ovolo**   **Quirk**

Molding profiles.

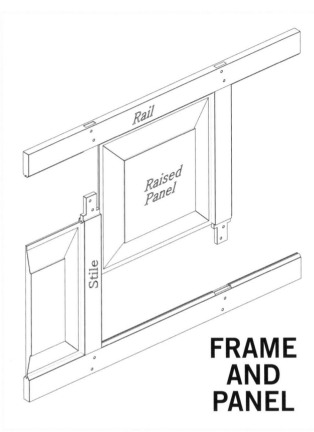

Rail

Raised Panel

Stile

FRAME AND PANEL

Quirk bead cut with a Stanley 45 molding plane.

Molding profiles were made from a few basic shapes. The convex "ovolo" profile was frequently used on Georgian period moldings, while the reverse curvature "ogee" profile was more popular on federal-period moldings. The "quirk" bead was used to finish edges on practically everything—baseboards, window casings, door panels, clapboards, and corner-boards. Quirk beads never went out of style. In my own shop, I have quirk bead router bits in a variety of sizes and they are all well used.

The material of choice for the joiner was clear, knot free, eastern white pine. It was easy to shape with hand planes and took paint well. Renovators will often spend thousands of hours stripping paint off pine millwork that was always intended to be painted.

Frame and panel construction was the trademark of the joiner. It was used for making doors, cabinets, wainscoting, and paneled walls. The frame was made of horizontal rails and vertical stiles joined with mortise and tenon joints. Grooves routed in the edges of the stiles and rails supported the panels. The panels could expand and contract freely with changes in moisture content without distorting the frame.

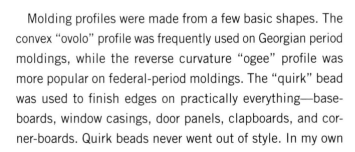

Carvings

Corner cupboards with scallop shell carved crowns were among the finest cabinets found in Georgian homes. They were used to display the homeowner's finest china.

Rose carved corner blocks frequently adorned door surrounds. The rose was a patriotic English symbol, much like the shamrock was to the Irish, or the thistle to the Scotts.

Rosettes were a way of saying "proud to be Englishmen."

Federal-period homes had carvings based on classical roman motifs such as acanthus leaves, garlands, and urns.

Carved scallop shell corner cupboard.

Rose carvings were patriotic symbols.

Carved acanthus leaf corner block.

Master Carver Mark Henion

Mark Henion with Deschenes and Cooper Architectural Millwork carves an Ionic pilaster capital from Honduran mahogany. Mark has a degree in art and apprentised as a furniture maker before becoming an architectural carver. He comes from a long line of woodworkers and still uses chisels and gouges handed down from his grandfather

Carver Mark Henion.

Fireplace Surrounds and Mantels

Georgian fireplace surrounds had no mantel shelf. The firebox was framed with a "bolection" molding. Mantels with a shelf and carved pilasters were a feature of federal- period homes.

Paneled fireplace wall with no mantel shelf. *Courtesy of Maurer & Shepherd.*

Bolection molding around fireplace.

Federal-period fireplace surround with a mantel shelf.

Stairs

Center chimney homes had narrow, steep stairs crowded between the front door and the chimney. The stairs often had pie-shaped winder treads with closed stringers and a simple handrail. The stairs were cramped but functional.

Center hall homes had stairs that were functional but also elegant, sometimes even grand. They featured open stringers and turned balusters.

Federal-period stairway.

Crowded stairway in a center chimney home.

Center hall stairway.

Early homes were not painted.

Throughout the seventeenth century and the first quarter of the eighteenth century, homes were left unpainted. It was not because people liked the look of bare wood; paint was just plain unavailable or prohibitively expensive. At first, only the wealthy could afford to paint their home, but by the mid-eighteenth century, most proper homes were painted.

Paint was not just for looking at. Unpainted wood exposed to the elements degrades and deteriorates much more rapidly than wood protected by paint.

In rural areas, painters were itinerant tradesmen who traveled from town to town. If you did not get your house painted when the painter was in town, you might not get

Bold yellow ochre color scheme. General John Ashley house, Ashley Falls, Massachusetts.

another chance for several years. Repainting was an infrequent activity. When a room was painted, it stayed that color for life.

There is a popular notion that colonial homes were always painted white on the exterior, but that is not true. Early homes were sometimes painted white but more often they were painted in color. The idea of painting all colonial houses white was a colonial revival thing from the twentieth century.

Most Georgian-period homes had a monochromatic color scheme on the exterior with the siding, windows, and trim painted the same color. On the interior, plaster walls and ceilings remained white and woodwork was painted in color. Federal-period homes were painted with contrasting colors. Greek revival homes were often painted white in an attempt to emulate the look of marble.

Paint Investigation

Before selecting a color scheme for your home, it is worthwhile to investigate what color paint was originally used. Paint conservators can use a number of sophisticated techniques to identify original paint colors, but you might want to try a simple technique yourself.

Select locations for paint sampling where it is least likely that the paint has been damaged, weathered, or removed. For instance, to sample exterior paint, your best bet is the north side of the house, behind a shutter. The only tools you will need are a sharp razor blade and a magnifying glass. Carefully cut through the paint, pivoting the blade to create a bulls-eye with the bare wood surface at the center. This is called a crater. Examining the crater with the magnifying glass, you can identify the various paint colors with the oldest near the center. Keep in mind that the oldest paint color may be a primer, not necessarily the finish paint, and also keep in mind that paint colors change with age. Pigments fade and linseed oil yellows. Paint conservators are capable

Paint crater.

of evaluating the aging effects on color and determine what the paint probably looked like in its day.

You are under no moral obligation to paint your home in the historically accurate colors if they do not appeal to you.

Paint Colors and Pigments

Most major paint producers today offer a line of historic paint colors, and a few smaller paint companies specialize in historic colors. You really can't go wrong with any of them. The paint colors tend to be muted and look appropriate on an antique house.

The authentic historic paint colors were actually brighter and more vivid than the muted colors that are offered as historic paints. It is only recently that the aging effects on paint colors have been understood, and the commercially available colors are based on older paint research that identified the color of paint that had faded and yellowed. If you choose to paint your house with brighter colors that are more authentic, you are likely to find that they look garish under good lighting. Old homes were originally dimly lit with candles that made bold colors look more subdued.

Early painters only had a small handful of color pigments to use in making their paints. They would blend and mill the pigments to produce a wide palette of colors. Their recipes for blending colors were a well-guarded secret. In seaport towns there were often paint makers called colourmen from which painters could buy premixed paint.

Milling pigments was time-consuming. Dry pigments were milled on a marble slab with a stone called a muller that was rotated on the slab. Linseed oil was added to the pigment as it was milled to produce a paste. The finer the pigments were milled, the more intense the colors.

White lead was probably the most important pigment. Not only could you make white paint with it, but it was also used as a base for colored pigments. White lead made an extremely durable paint for the exterior of homes. It was used up until the 1970s when it was banned due to health issues. In modern paints, titanium dioxide is commonly used instead of white lead, but it is not nearly as durable.

Earth pigments were the most common, affordable, and versatile. They were mined from clay soils whose color was imparted by the iron in the soil. Red iron-oxide pigment also went by the name red ochre, Spanish brown, and Venetian red. It was used commonly as a primer paint and also as a finish paint in utility spaces such as kitchens or for the outside of a barn.

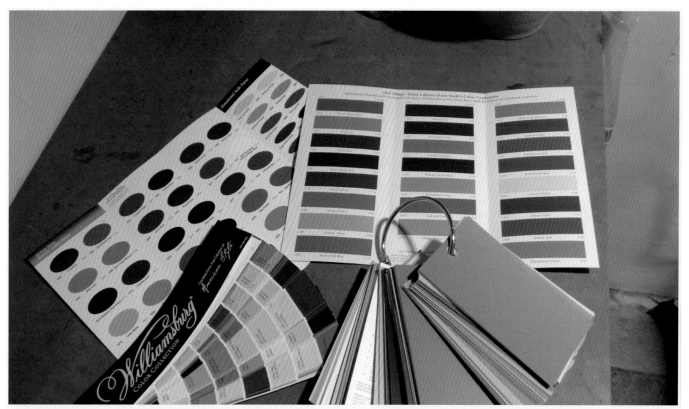

Broad selection of historic paint colors.

Parlor painted in Prussian Blue, Eastfield Village.

Chapter Twenty-Five: Paint and Paper | **Part Three**

Yellow ochre, also called raw sienna, raw umber, and burnt umber were other common earth pigments for yellow and brown paints. As the name implies, earth pigments were the color of soil and sometimes looked muddy. They were not considered elegant enough for the finest room in the house.

Prussian blue was a chemically synthesized pigment imported from Berlin. It was expensive and typically reserved for painting the parlor where you wanted to show off.

Verdigris was another expensive pigment. It was blue-green in color and made from corroded copper. It was not a stable pigment and would sometimes turn black with age.

Indigo was a much more affordable blue pigment. It was an organic pigment made from the indigo plant and more commonly used to dye fabric. As is typical of organic pigments, it tended to fade with age. Indigo was often used as a pigment for milk paint.

Probably the most under-appreciated pigment was lamp black. As the name suggests, it is a carbon pigment made from the soot of oil lamps. While black paint was not particularly popular, lamp black was blended with white lead to make gray paint. It was also frequently blended with color pigments to produce more muted tones. Lamp black is the tinting color that I use most frequently to fine- tune the shade of store mixed paints.

Pigment was sold in bulk.

Linseed Oil Paints

Linseed oil paints were used on interior and exterior woodwork. They were the best and most expensive paints of their day. Linseed oil was blended with pigment, natural resin varnish, and turpentine, to produce the paint.

Brush marks are noticeable in linseed oil paint surfaces. The resulting ropey surface texture is distinctive.

When exposed to sunlight the ultraviolet rays will cause the linseed oil to degrade. This results in the surface chalking. Paint manufacturers once marketed chalking paint as an asset. They called it self-cleaning paint since rain would wash away dirt along with the chalked paint surface. In reality, the paint film was slowly eroding away.

Linseed oil will yellow with age unless exposed to sunlight. Consequently, it holds its color well until it is overpainted, fooling later paint researchers.

Modern oil-based paints use alkyd resins instead of linseed oil and perform much better. There is no good reason to use linseed oil paint today unless you are a purist and enjoy torturing yourself.

Milk Paints

Milk paint, also referred to as casein paint, was an inexpensive paint that could be made at home. It was a blend of skim milk, lime, and pigment. Don't try it yourself, as I have never met anybody who had success getting the recipe right. Only earth pigments or indigo were used with milk paint since the lime would react with other pigments.

It was a thin, watery paint that produced a flat, semi-transparent film. Several paint companies today sell what they call milk paint. One comes in a powder form that you mix with water; the others are just thin, flat, acrylic paints. I suspect that there isn't actually any milk in any of them, but it doesn't really matter since they do resemble milk paint.

Real milk paint cannot be removed with chemical paint removers. If you are stripping paint and hit a layer that just won't budge, odds are it is milk paint.

Imitation milk paint can be purchased in powder form or premixed.

Limewash

You have probably read the story of Tom Sawyer whitewashing the fence and wondered, what the heck is whitewash anyway? Whitewash, also called limewash, has been in use since prehistoric times to coat masonry, plaster, and wood. Technically it is not a paint at all, more like a thin coating of lime plaster. It is made from slaked lime putty thinned with water to the consistency of milk.

If you are tempted to mix up a batch of limewash from powdered hydrated lime—don't! It won't work—it has to be slaked lime putty.

Although limewash can be tinted with earth pigments, the rule was "you can get it in any color, as long as it is white." It was commonly used to coat interior plaster or wattle and daub walls, timber ceilings, stone cellar walls, and barn siding.

Limewashed ceiling.

Limewash has antiseptic properties due to its high alkalinity. For sanitary reasons, the inside of barns were sometimes limewashed because it was believed to inhibit the spread of diseases such as bovine tuberculosis.

Calcimine Paint

If you have sheets of paint peeling off of your ceiling, odds are you have calcimine paint. Calcimine paint is the scourge of home restorers.

Calcimine paint was the original water-based paint. Also called distemper paint, it only came in white and was used on plaster ceilings until the 1950s. It was made of chalk pigment, also called whiting, hide glue, and water.

There is nothing wrong with calcimine paint until you try to paint over it. Paint will not stick to it. Calcimine paint is water soluble and can be washed off the ceiling with soap, water, and a lot of elbow grease, provided nobody has tried to paint over it before you. If there is peeling paint over the calcimine paint, your worst restoration nightmare is about

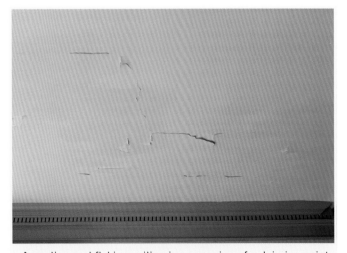
A peeling and flaking ceiling is a sure sign of calcimine paint.

to begin. You must remove both the calcimine paint and the paint on top of it. The only technique I have found that is effective at removing the paint is a wallpaper steamer and a scraper. To describe it as a dirty, unpleasant project is an understatement. If you try to just scrape off the loose, peeling paint and paint over it without removing everything first, the fresh paint will start bubbling and hanging from the ceiling even before it dries and you will have an even bigger mess on your hands.

If you are not up for removing the old paint, there is an easier way. The sure-fire cure is to cover the ceiling with sheetrock. As long as there are no crown moldings around the ceiling, this is a pretty painless solution. The only downside is that the ceiling might end up looking too new for an antique house.

Another technique I have used is to scrape off the peeling paint and skim coat the entire ceiling with joint compound with a mesh reinforcement. Fiberglass insect screen makes a good reinforcement. I can't guarantee that it will work for you, but it has worked for me.

Paint Stripping and Surface Preparation

The success of any painting project relies on good surface preparation. For painting exterior wood siding, nothing beats taking it down to bare wood and giving it a fresh coat of alkyd-based primer with acrylic topcoats, particularly if you have multiple layers of peeling and failing paint.

There are several paint removal methods to choose from— power sanding, heat guns, scraping, and chemical paint removers. Each one of these methods has the potential for damaging your home as well as the person using them. You must weigh the risks and pick your poison.

For my own home, I chose to remove the exterior paint by sandblasting. It seemed like a good idea at the time, but it turned out to be a huge mistake. The sandblasting eroded my 200-year-old wood shingles, rounded over the crisp edges on the trim work, and pitted some of the window glass.

It was thirty-five years ago and I chalk it up to having been young and stupid. I am now older and wiser. I have since removed the damaged sidewall shingles and replaced them. I can't do much about the damaged trim; I just try not to look at it.

Interior woodwork is a different situation. If the old paint is in good condition, all that is needed is a light sanding before repainting. There is usually no need to embark on a major paint-stripping project, and it is best to preserve the paint history. That is, unless you have a serious lead problem.

Painting over failed paint is foolish.

Sandblasting my house was a really bad idea.

Lead Remediation

It is unusual to find an antique home that does not contain some lead-based paint. I expect to find it everywhere on painted woodwork and am seldom disappointed. Lead paint can be a health hazard to young children, pregnant women, and to a lesser extent adults. The risk is greatest if you breathe in paint dust from power-sanding or if you are in the habit of eating paint chips. If you have a serious lead paint hazard, a major paint stripping project may be in your future.

You can buy lead paint test kits at the hardware store, but it is more reliable to have your paint tested by a professional, particularly if you have small children. There are regulations in place that dictate how you must handle lead-based paint in your home. Remodeling contractors are required to be trained and certified to deal with lead paint. You have to follow the letter of the law—this is not something you want to screw around with.

Color Layering and Distressing

A good painter will spend endless hours flattening walls and sanding woodwork smooth, eradicating all dings and blemishes prior to painting. He will tint the primer to match the topcoat and apply a smooth coat of paint with no trace of lumps or brush marks. The final results will be flawless, but a little too perfect for my taste.

I sometimes prefer to leave the imperfections and celebrate the battle scars of age. I will even go so far as to intentionally distress the paint to give the look of an antique surface on my antique home.

The first step is to layer the colors. The primer paint should contrast with the color of the topcoat. I usually go with a dark red primer paint similar to the color of an old red ochre paint. After the topcoat has dried, I sand it lightly with an extra fine sandpaper in places where natural wear would occur, such as at corners and around knobs or latches. Sanding with a light touch will expose just a hint of the color below the surface. It takes some practice to achieve a naturally distressed look, but if you mess up you can always paint over it and try again.

Cupboard with lightly distressed paint finish.

Flowering tree stencil painting inspired by a design by Lyn Le Grice.

Stenciling designs on a plaster wall was a good way to cheer up a drab interior. Stencil and mural painters were itinerant artists that traveled from town to town offering their services. The most well-known itinerant wall artists of the early nineteenth century were Moses Eaton, Rufus Porter, and Jonathan Poor. Stenciling was much more affordable than imported wallpaper and considerably less ostentatious.

Stencil painting has experienced a revival and there are a variety of precut stencils and stencil paints readily available today. You no longer need to wait for a stencil painter to come to town; you can do it yourself. My wife is a talented artist and has adorned our home with some marvelous stencil painting.

Floral stencil, Eastfield Village.

Faux Finishes

Painting wood surfaces to look like more expensive materials was very fashionable. Doors and paneled walls were grain painted to look like mahogany, columns were faux painted to look like marble, and exterior wood siding was sometimes made to look like cut stone.

Trompe l'oeil fireboard with faux marble border hand painted by my talented wife, Vera. *Suzanne Sheridan Photography.*

Grain painted door, Eastfield Village.

Wallpaper

Wallpaper was reserved for only the wealthiest homes. It was imported mostly from France and the selection of designs was limited. Measured by today's taste, it was a bit gaudy, unless you happen to like it.

Wallpaper was printed by hand with carved wood blocks until 1837 when a machine was patented for printing wallpaper. By 1840, machine-made wallpaper became affordable and found its way into less affluent homes.

Some wallpapers produced in the mid-nineteenth century contain arsenic in the ink, particularly dark green inks. Dust from the wallpaper can be unhealthy to breath. Most people do not think to test their wallpaper to see if it is dangerous.

This pineapple motif wallpaper is not historically correct, but it looks appropriate.

Authentic wallpaper.

Chapter Twenty-Six
BLOOD AND GUTS—PLUMBING, ELECTRICAL, AND HVAC SYSTEMS

When my home was built in 1809, their idea of indoor plumbing was hauling buckets of water from the well and emptying the chamber pot, electricity was some crazy thing that Ben Franklin did with a kite, and central heat was the fire in the central fireplace. That suited everybody just fine for over a century. Then, in 1930, the house was purchased by an affluent young couple accustomed to the finer things in life. They remodeled and modernized the house with indoor plumbing, electrical wiring, and steam heat. At the time, those building systems were not considered necessities; they were luxuries.

A half-century later, I acquired the house. The luxurious plumbing, electrical, and heating systems from 1930 were still operational, but functionally obsolete. It was time for a complete overhaul. Antique homes have a reputation for being high maintenance because the support systems are usually past their prime and have never been upgraded. When planning a restoration project, fix the stuff that nobody sees before you spend a nickel on the stuff that shows.

When it comes to older plumbing, electrical wiring, and heating systems, my motto is, "when in doubt—rip it out."

Plumbing

Water piping is the circulatory system of a house and the waste pipes are the bowels. With age, water pipes become brittle and choked with plaque. The only remedy is to replace the piping. If you have brass pipes with threaded fittings, the situation is terminal. If you have lead pipes, the situation is dangerous. Unless badly corroded, copper piping with soldered fittings is probably repairable, although the solder may contain lead. A water test will determine if you have a lead contamination issue.

Older drain, waste, and vent (DWV) pipes are usually cast iron with lead joints. This is a durable type of pipe that can last a century. The lead joints do not present any health issues unless you are drinking the sewage, in which case you have bigger issues. If the cast iron has not rusted through, it can

This timber beam was butchered to accommodate a waste pipe.

probably remain in service. Galvanized or lead pipes should be replaced.

Modern water pipes are made of cross-linked polyethylene (PEX) or copper. DWV piping is usually made of polyvinyl chloride (PVC) or cast iron. As you probably have guessed, PEX is a lot cheaper than copper and PVC is cheaper than cast iron.

I usually don't find old plumbing fixtures particularly charming, but if you love the look of your old fixtures, they can probably be refurbished, but it is unlikely that the old faucets and hardware can be saved. For my money, it is smarter to go with new fixtures.

Timber frame houses were not built with plumbing pipes in mind. Often, structural timbers are located exactly where a plumber wants to put his pipes. One of the laws of classical physics states that two objects cannot occupy the same space at the same time. When there is competition between a timber and a pipe to occupy a space, the pipe usually wins. Plumbers can be ruthless when it comes to butchering structural timbers. In my professional practice, I have seen more structural damage caused by plumbers than by termites. I am not suggesting that we should exterminate plumbers; I am just saying that we should take their Sawzalls away.

The antique plumbing fixtures in my home were not charming.

Knob and tube wiring is dangerous.

Antiquated electrical wiring is not just inconvenient, it can be downright dangerous, particularly knob and tube wiring. Knob and tube wiring was popular from 1880 to 1930. The wires were not enclosed in a protective sheathing and were nailed to the wood framing with porcelain knobs. Where the wires passed through the framing, porcelain tubes prevented the wires from touching the wood. The systems were not grounded and the insulation on the wires becomes brittle and frayed with age. Knob and tube wiring will turn any house into a fire trap. If you find it in your house, don't even think about keeping it.

Armored cable, called BX cable, replaced knob and tube wiring by 1930. While BX is considerably safer than knob and tube, it does have issues. The armored sheathing serves as the ground conductor and it is not a very reliable ground. Modern armored cable, called MC cable, looks like BX but has a separate ground wire inside. As with knob and tube, the wire insulation inside BX cable can become brittle and frayed, particularly at light fixtures where the heat from the light can accelerate the deterioration of the insulation.

The most popular electrical cable used today is plastic sheathed cable, called NM cable, or Romex. If your house has Romex wiring, you don't need to be overly concerned about the condition of the wiring. You still need to make sure that the individual who put the wiring in knew what he was doing. Romex is so easy to work with in that it tends to invite amateur electricians, and they can be just as dangerous as old wiring.

Most older electrical services are rated at sixty amp capacity. Today, 200 amps is considered a reasonable minimum rating for an electrical service. If your electrical service is rated for less than 200 amps, upgrading is a good idea.

In older systems, circuits were protected with fuses. Fuses are no longer considered reliable circuit protectors. If you have a fuse box, it is a good idea to convert the system over to circuit breakers.

Rewiring can be a fairly simple, straightforward project if you have gutted the plaster out of the house first. If you are leaving the plaster walls and ceilings undisturbed, rewiring is a bit more challenging and expensive. The difference between a good electrician and a mediocre electrician is not the way that they connect the wires, it is the way that they snake wires in a wall or ceiling. A skilled electrician can magically get new wires inside a wall or ceiling with no signs that he was ever there. A less skilled electrician will leave behind holes in the plaster everywhere for you to patch, and he won't stop complaining about it. It is worth it to pay a little more for a craftsman.

Heating and Air Conditioning

When I purchased my home, it was heated by a steam boiler that was originally coal fired. It had two iron doors on the front where the coal had been shoveled in. There was still a bin full of anthracite coal in the basement left over from the coal burning days. The boiler had been converted to fuel oil decades before by sticking an oil burner through a hole cut into one of the coal doors. I estimated that its efficiency was comparable to tossing a bucket of fuel oil onto a camp fire. The boiler was larger than my car and slathered with asbestos insulation.

There were steam radiators in every room that performed a chorus of hissing and clanging whenever the heat came on, which was often. Some people love

An oil-fired boiler past its prime.

the look of old radiators—I am not one of them. After living with the steam system for one winter, I knew it had to go and I have no regrets about tearing it out and replacing it with an efficient gas-fired boiler.

I did make one major mistake. I chalk it up to being young and stupid. I thought that I really did not need air-conditioning. So I put in a whole new hydronic heating system without any provisions for cooling. A couple of years later, after I moved my office into the house, I realized what an incredibly stupid decision that had been. After spending a summer dripping sweat all over my drawing board, I put in central air.

The most comfortable way to both heat and cool a house is with a forced air system. Shoehorning ductwork into an antique house can be a challenge. I put in two separate systems. I have one air-handler in the basement that serves the first floor, with ductwork in the basement and floor registers. The second air-handler is in the attic and serves the second floor, with ductwork in the attic and ceiling diffusers. The gas-fired boiler in the basement feeds hot water to both air-handlers. This is a practical solution for heating and cooling an old house, unless you have a finished basement or attic, in which case you are screwed.

If your old house has a heating system that is more than thirty years old, it is probably not operating very efficiently. There are a lot of high-efficiency heating and cooling systems on the market today—geothermal systems, modulating boilers, mini-split heat pumps, to name a few. The technology is changing at a rapid pace. Systems that were considered state-of-the-art a few years ago are now considered yesterday's news. Any of these high-efficiency systems can be adapted to an antique house if you are feeling adventurous. Reasonably efficient, time-tested systems are sometimes a less risky choice.

Heating with Wood

Antique homes were once heated by burning wood in the fireplaces. This fact has misled many homeowners to believe that they can save energy by using their fireplaces—nothing could be further from the truth. The moment you open the damper and build a fire, you begin sucking heated air out of the house and up the flue at an alarming rate.

If you have done a good job of insulating and air-sealing your house, there is a good chance that the fireplace won't even work and will promptly fill the house with smoke. For an average-size fireplace to maintain a proper draft, you need approximately 300 cubic feet per minute (CFM) of outside air coming into the house. A large fireplace may need twice that volume of fresh air. A drafty, uninsulated, old house usually has sufficient air infiltration for the fireplaces to function, but well-insulated houses seldom do.

So if your fireplace smokes, what can you do? You have two choices. You can either put in a mechanical make-up air system that sucks outside air into the house and pre-heats it, or you can open a window. Both solutions will work, and they will both consume about the same amount of energy. You don't have to give up the experience of a wood fire,

Woodstoves are an efficient way to heat the house.

just open a window, crank up the thermostat, and enjoy the romance.

It is possible to efficiently heat with wood, just not in the fireplace. Woodstoves are a marvelous way to heat. Nothing warms your bones on a cold day better than standing in front of a woodstove. But don't stick a woodstove inside your fireplace and vent it into your brick chimney flue. For a woodstove to work efficiently and safely, it should have its own insulated metal flue sized to match the stove.

I heat with my woodstove all winter long. The room where the stove is located used to get too hot and dry. I solved that problem by putting the return-air intake for my central heating system directly behind the stove. The air-handler draws the hot air from behind the stove and distributes it throughout the first floor.

A crackling fire can be romantic.

Chapter Twenty-Seven
LANDSCAPES, GARDENS, AND GROUNDS

I would prefer the delights of a garden to the dominion of a world.

—John Adams

The Changing Landscape

When the Separatists landed at Plymouth, they viewed the New England forest as a vast, frightening wilderness, full of demons, wild animals, and heathen savages. In reality, the forests had been tamed and managed by the Native Americans for centuries. The Wampanoags lived in villages, raised crops in clearings, fished the estuaries, and hunted game in the forests. They periodically burned the forest understory to open up the forest for better hunting. English cod fisherman had been visiting the New England coast for decades and traded regularly with the natives. The Native Americans had no natural resistance to European diseases contracted from contact with the English, and their population had been decimated by a

The wild and woody forest.

smallpox epidemic. The Separatists had the good fortune of inheriting cleared fields that had recently been abandoned by the epidemic victims. They were startled when the first heathen savage that they encountered spoke fluent English.

Throughout the seventeenth and eighteenth centuries, new townships and farmsteads spread throughout New England. At first, small clearings were created around a farmstead to raise crops and pasture animals, but also to push the edge of the wilderness back. Trees were felled, stumps

pulled, and brush burned. Water powered sawmills turned the felled trees into building materials for barns and farmhouses. Every year the edge of the scary wilderness was pushed back a little farther and the farmlands expanded.

By 1800, there was no wilderness left. Native Americans had been evicted from the land over a century earlier. The vast forests had been reduced to small woodlots surrounded by open fields. Agriculture in New England was prospering. Prior generations had cleared the land and energy could now be devoted to tending the farm. With prosperity came more elegant living conditions. Ramshackle cabins were replaced by stylish homes.

Following the Civil War, farming in New England declined. The Erie Canal, western expansion, and the railroads contributed to the decline. Crops could be raised more efficiently in Ohio and shipped east. The New England farms could not compete. Farms were soon abandoned and the mill towns grew. It wasn't long before the forests reclaimed the land.

New England Towns

The settlement pattern in New England took the form of a mosaic of towns, each with its own center. A town was established when a land grant was bestowed on a handful of proprietors who would become the town founders. Each proprietor would be granted a modest house plot adjacent to a common town green. The common provided communal pasture for livestock and a place to muster the militia. A meetinghouse with a burying ground would be prominently sited on the green. The meetinghouse was not just a church, it was also the center of local government. Each of the proprietors was also granted sizable acreage beyond the town center for establishing a farm.

The clustering of homes in a town center was intended to facilitate defense from hostile natives and also to foster a close bond with the church. However, it proved to be impractical and inefficient for farming. Within a generation, homes were being built remote from town centers, adjacent to farm fields and pastures.

Town centers did not develop into active community centers until the late eighteenth century. Town centers then became places for conducting business. Roads connecting town centers became turnpikes with regular stagecoach service. With farms prospering and producing surpluses, New Englanders found themselves with disposable income. Shops,

Town Green, Litchfield, Connecticut.

Field with a flag pole is reminiscent of a town green.

taverns, and markets made the town green a happening place. In addition to a meetinghouse, town centers now had a courthouse, which meant that you also needed a lawyer in town. Doctors' offices were established, as well as an assortment of artisans, maybe even a mill or two.

The nuclear village with antique homes huddled around a town green has become one of the most picturesque and charming characteristics of the New England landscape.

Farmsteads

Most antique homes were built at the heart of a farm, not fronting a town green. The core of a farm was a campus of buildings—a farmhouse, barn, corn crib, chicken coop, woodshed, wagon shed, hay rick, work shed, and outhouse. It was not a neat, manicured campus—it was a messy and smelly place with buildings that appeared to be haphazardly positioned. There were no trim lawns, although there was plenty of grass that was kept mown by sheep.

Fields for raising crops were sited on the fertile bottomlands adjacent to a stream or river. The rocky hillsides became hay fields and pastures for grazing. Rocks cleared from the fields were piled around the perimeter to keep animals in or out. The stone walls partitioned the land into a patchwork of rectangular fields, each with a designated function.

Rows of trees grew along the fence lines, creating a wind break. Apple trees bordered the lanes and paths. A woodlot of forest trees was maintained for harvesting firewood, building materials, and maple sugar. Some coastal farms were fortunate to have salt marshes with spartina grasses for winter fodder.

New Englanders practiced mixed agriculture. They planted a variety of crops. If one crop failed, they were not ruined and would not starve. They raised milk cows, oxen, hogs, chickens, and sheep. Sometimes even a horse or two.

Cows pasturing on the hills.

Farms were not tidy, manicured landscapes.

Besides farming, they also practiced a trade. They were coopers, cobblers, bakers, furniture makers, tinsmiths, and blacksmiths to make a little extra cash or barter in their spare time. Farms were extremely diversified operations. Later, midwestern farms were much more specialized, often producing a single crop—but a lot of it.

Barns were sited apart from the farmhouse so that fire could not spread from the barn to the house. Barns filled with hay were always a fire risk. If hay was not completely dried before being put away, the heat from decomposition could cause it to spontaneously ignite. The area in front of the barn was the barnyard where many of the farm chores were done, such as splitting wood, shoveling manure, and castrating bulls. Farming was hard, dirty work.

Amidst all of the noise, smells, and chaos of the farm, there was one place where beauty, order, and sweet fragrances reined. It was a place of solitude where the woman of the house could feel like a lady—the garden.

Freeman farm barnyard, Old Sturbridge Village.

Dooryard Garden

The dooryard garden was at the front of the house and you passed through it to get to the entry. It was enclosed with a picket fence and gate to keep out farm animals. The space between the pickets was made narrower than the breadth of a chicken.

Brick or gravel paths in a geometric pattern bordered planting beds of herbs and flowers. A medley of annual and perennial flowers gave color and fragrance to the garden.

Herbs were grown for their utilitarian function. Culinary herbs such as parsley, sage, rosemary, and thyme gave flavor to gristley foods. Household herbs included indigo used to dye cloth and flax, which was used to make into linen and paint. A variety of medicinal herbs could be made into teas, potions, and concoctions for whatever ailed you. Some of the home remedies actually worked while others were merely based on superstition.

Dooryard garden.

Chives is a culinary herb that adds color to the garden.

Whipple house garden, Ipswich, Massachusetts.

A cottage garden.

Cottage gardens were similar to dooryard gardens—they were just messier. Tall flowers were planted close together in a random fashion that crowded out weeds to create a look of organized chaos.

The dooryard garden was a source of pride and a place of delight. It also functioned as a charming and civilized place to greet visitors.

Kitchen Garden

The kitchen garden was devoted to food production and was somewhat less fancy than the dooryard garden. Vegetables, root crops, and herbs were grown there. The kitchen door opened directly into the garden and there was also direct access from the garden into the cellar, where the bountiful harvest was stored over the winter. To maximize sunlight, the kitchen garden was typically on the south side of the house.

Plants were grown in heavily manured, rectangular, raised beds. Narrow paths between the beds allowed the plants to be cultivated without having to step into the beds. The kitchen garden was built for function, not for beauty. The fence enclosing the garden was made of crude palings or rough boards. The paths were made of gravel or stepping stones.

Kitchen garden, Old Sturbridge Village.

Fruit Trees and Orchards

Every farm needed fruit trees—particularly apples and pears. Although entire fields were sometimes planted as orchards with neat rows of trees, more frequently fruit trees were planted alongside lanes and around the perimeter of farm fields. Occasionally a pair of pear trees would be planted within a dooryard garden.

Apples were an important crop. Although some of the apples were eaten, most were destined for the cider press. Hard cider was a popular beverage that kept all year long and was safer to drink than water from shallow wells that were easily contaminated.

On my own property in Warren, I have a dozen gnarly old apple trees scattered around the perimeter of what had once been a farm field. When I found them, they were down on

their luck, crowded, and shaded by second-growth maples that moved in after the farm was abandoned in 1960. The apple trees were near death and had not produced apples in decades. I cleared away the maples and nursed them back to health by pruning their limbs and sweetening the soil with a heavy dose of lime. A few just did not have the strength to go on and I had to put them out of their misery with my chain saw. The rest are now thriving and are covered with apples in the fall. While I never found picking out apples at the supermarket to be much of a thrill, plucking apples from these tough, old survivors is fun. I am not much for hard cider, but my wife makes a mean apple pie that just can't be beat.

Apples are vulnerable to a host of pests, diseases, and fungus that can blemish the fruit. Commercial growers make a habit of frequently spraying apple trees to protect them. The sprays are toxic and can be harmful to wildlife. It is not uncommon for the soil to be contaminated with dangerous levels of arsenic where orchards once grew. I prefer to not spray and take my chances. Spots on the apples don't bother me, and the birds are happier for it.

Apple trees lined the lanes.

Apple pie baking in a beehive oven.

Natural Gardens

Originally inspired by medieval monastery gardens, formal geometric gardens were the fashion throughout the seventeenth and eighteenth centuries. They symbolized the taming of nature and conquering of the wilderness. In the nineteenth century, the winds of fashion began to blow in a different direction. Natural gardens became the rage. Nature no longer needed to be tamed; it was to be celebrated. The forests had long since been cleared and were now crop fields and pastures. Nobody could even remember when there was a wilderness.

Trees were planted in informal groupings and underplanted with clumps of ferns, perennials, and annuals. Gardens emulated natural woodlands and meadows. Rock outcrops, streams, and ponds were now delightful features. Serpentine strolling paths wandered through the landscape and gardens.

A natural woodland garden.

Period Plants

Visit any garden nursery in the spring and you will find a wide selection of flowers, trees, and shrubs from around the world. Modern technology has produced new plant varieties by cross breeding, hybridizing, and grafting. But if you are trying to reproduce a period garden, many of the new and improved plant species just don't look right.

Native New England plants dominated early gardens. Some were wildflowers that grew in meadows while others were herbs that had been cultivated by Native Americans. Early New England gardeners treasured the familiar plants from England and brought seeds with them to plant in their new home. While some of the imported seeds thrived, others proved ill-suited to the climate.

In the eighteenth century, it became fashionable in England to have American flowers in your garden. Seeds were crossing the Atlantic in both directions. The practice of importing exotic plant species from other parts of the world has never gone out of fashion. In some cases the consequences were disastrous. Asian chestnut trees imported to America in the late nineteenth century harbored a blight fungus that decimated the American chestnut trees.

Every garden had a lilac.

Period Plant Species

Balloon flower *(Platycodon grandifloras)*
Beebalm *(Monarda didyma)*
Bellflower *(Campanula sp.)*
Chives *(Allium schoenoprasum)*
Columbine *(Aquilegia vulgaris)*
Coreopsis *(Coreopsis lanceolate)*
Cutleaf coneflower *(Rudbeckia laciniata)*
Daffodil *(Narcissus* sp.)
Daylily *(Hemerocallis* sp.)
Dill *(Anetheum graveolens)*
Evening primrose *(Oenothera biennis)*
Flax *(Linum perenne)*
Foxglove *(Digitalis purpurea)*
Garlic *(Allium sativum)*

Hollyhock *(Althae rosea)*
Iris *(Iris* sp.)
Johnny-jump-up *(Viola tricolor)*
Lavender *(Lavandula vera)*
Mallow *(Malva alcea)*
Parsley *(Petroselinum filicinum)*
Purple coneflower *(Echinacea purpurea)*
Rosemary *(Rosmarinus officinalis)*
Sage *(Salvia officinalis)*
Sweet William, pinks *(Dianthus sp.)*
Thyme *(Thymus vulgaris)*
Wild geranium *(Geranium sp.)*
Yarrow *(Achillea milefolium)*

Some plants had preferred locations in the garden. Lilac shrubs were often planted near a corner of the house, while hollyhocks were planted around the outhouse to screen it from view and add a different fragrance.

The plant species listed are similar to those that would have been grown in early gardens and look appropriate in a reproduced period garden. I have included only plants that I like and that are readily available at garden centers. If you are a purist and do not want to settle for readily available plants, there are sources for antique and heirloom plant seeds if you don't mind hunting for them.

Linen was made from the stalk of the flax plant and linseed oil for paint was made from its seeds.

Stone Walls and Fences

When you think of the New England landscape, images of stone walls and picket fences come to mind. Clearing stones from fields was an endless chore for early New Englanders hacking a farm out of the wilderness. The stones were dumped around the perimeter of the fields, forming crude stone walls to keep animals in or out. It was not until the early nineteenth century that Yankee farmers had the time and inclination to lay the stones as neat, straight walls. Today the forests have reclaimed the fields, but the network of stone walls running through the woods is a reminder

Stone walls that once bordered farm fields now ramble through the forest.

A scroll-top gate and a picket fence enclose the dooryard.

Elaborate picket fence with urn topped posts, Bennington, Vermont.

A zig-zag Virginia rail fence was a quick way to enclose a field without the need for digging fence post holes.

that the forested landscape was once croplands and pastures.

Picket fences enclosed the dooryard garden by the house. They were sometimes whitewashed, but more often they were not painted at all. If they were painted, they would typically be painted the same color as the house.

These marvelous reproduction homes are in a suburban setting, complete with a cul-de-sac.

Like most antique homes, my home still stands on the same site and location where it was built over 200 years ago. But the setting is no longer the same. The house once stood along-side a country road and commanded a prosperous hundred-acre onion farm that stretched down to the river. Today the country road is a busy state road with a traffic light in front of the house and an interstate highway within earshot. The farm was subdivided over a century ago and the house now sits on a half-acre lot surrounded by post-war suburban homes.

The challenge is to create a setting for your antique home that is appropriate to the period of the house. You spent a lot of time and money restoring your antique house; you can't just stop at the front door. The landscape needs to be reminiscent of the original setting. It would be nice to re-route the highway and bulldoze the suburban homes in the neighborhood, but that is not a re-alistic expectation for most people.

Increasingly urbanized setting.

Suburban landscaping with stately front lawns and foun-dation plantings crowded against the house don't look right in front of an antique house. Period gardens with stone walls and picket fences are a much better idea.

The garage is around back and disguised as a carriage house.

Blacktop driveways leading straight to a garage with prominent overhead doors facing the road don't enhance the setting, either. If you must have a garage, put it in the back and disguise it as a barn or carriage house. Gravel drives with stone borders that meander to their destination fit in much better than blacktop runways.

Think of the landscape as a setting in which to display your antique home.

Epilogue
ZEN AND THE ART OF LIVING WITH YOUR ANTIQUE HOME

Maybe it cost you a lot more than you thought it would. Maybe there were times when you wished that you had never started the whole thing. But when I look around at what you two have got here . . . maybe there are some things you should buy with your heart, not your head. Maybe those are the things that really count.

—Melvyn Douglas, from the motion picture *Mr. Blandings Builds His Dream House*, 1948

Now that you have survived the restoration of your home, assuming that your spouse has not left you and you are not now financially destitute, what do you do next? There is only one thing to do—enjoy it.

Accept the fact that you have become a custodian rather than a homeowner, and that you now have a duty to lovingly care for your home so that it can be passed on to future generations. You may just find that you could never live anywhere else and going away on vacation isn't as much fun as it used to be because those charming country getaways aren't as charming as home.

Just try not to gloat too much to your poor friends who have to live in newer homes.

Cheers!

Suzanne Sheridan Photography.

FURTHER READING

Cummings, Abbott Lowell. *The Framed Houses of Massachusetts Bay, 1625-1725.* Cambridge, MA: Harvard University Press, 1979.

Endersby, Elric, Alexander Greenwood, and David Larkin. *Barn—The Art of a Working Building.* New York: Houghton Mifflin Company, 1992.

Garvin, James L. *A Building History of Northern New England.* Hanover, NH: University Press of New England, 2001.

Hubka, Thomas C. *Big House, Little House, Back House, Barn—The Connected Farm Buildings of New England.* Hanover, NH: University Press of New England, 1984.

Isham, Norman M., and Albert F. Brown. *Early Connecticut Houses—An Historical and Architectural Study.* Originally published in 1900; reprinted by Dover Publications, New York, 1965.

Kauffman, Henry J. *Metalworking Trades in Early America.* Originally published 1966; reprinted by Astragal Press, Mendham, NJ, 1995.

Kelly, J. Frederick. *Early Domestic Architecture of Connecticut.* Originally published in 1924; reprinted by Schiffer Publishing, Atglen, PA, 2007.

Knudsen, Jeff. *Design and Build a Great Eighteenth-Century Room.* Atglen, PA: Schiffer Publishing 2001

Kornwolf, James D. *Architecture and Town Planning in Colonial North America (3 volume set).* Baltimore: John Hopkins University Press, 2002.

Moss, Roger W. *Paint in America—The Colors of Historic Buildings.* Washington, DC: The Preservation Press, 1994.

Nash, George. *Renovating Old Houses.* Newtown, CT: The Taunton Press, 2003.

Richmond, Arthur P. *The Evolution of the Cape Cod House.* Atglen, PA: Schiffer Publishing, 2011.

Sloane, Eric. *A Reverence for Wood.* Originally published 1965; reprinted by Dover Publications, New York, 2004.

Sobon, Jack A. *Historic American Timber Joinery.* Becket, MA: Timber Framers Guild, 2002.

Sonn, Albert H. *Early American Wrought Iron.* Originally published 1928; reprinted by Bonanza Books, New York, 1989.

Tyler, Norman, Ted J. Ligibel, and Irene R. Tyler. *Historic Preservation.* New York: W. W. Norton & Company, 2009.

Underhill, Roy. *The Woodwright's Shop—A Practical Guide to Traditional Woodcraft.* Chapel Hill, NC: University of North Carolina Press, 1981.

RESOURCES

Restoration Contractors

Early New England Restorations
25 White Rock Road
Pawcatuck, CT 06379
www.thecoopergroupct.com
860-599-4393

R. J. Aley Building Contractor
185 Wilton Road
Westport, CT 06880
www.rjaley.com
203-221-9933

Millwork

Maurer & Shepherd Joyners
22 Naubuc Avenue
Glastonbury, CT 06033
www.msjoyners.com
860-633-2393

Deschenes & Cooper Architectural Millwork
25 White Rock Road
Pawcatuck, CT 06379
www.thecoopergroupct.com
860-599-2481

Timber Framers

Joe Turco
New England Timber Framers
Westerly, RI 02891
www.netimberframers.com
401-932-2439

Preservation Timber Framing, Inc.
P.O. Box 28
77 Berwick Road
Berwick, ME 03901
www.preservationtimberframing.com
207-698-1695

South County Post and Beam
521 Liberty Lane
West Kingston, RI 02892
www.scpb.com
401-783-4415

Stone Masons

Stonewalls by George
P.O. Box 2306
New Preston, CT 06777
www.stonewallsbygeorge.com
860-868-0903

Dendrochronology Dating

Bill Flynt, Architectural Conservator
Historic Deerfield, Inc.
wflynt@historic-deerfield.org
413-775-7210

Traditional Crafts & Trades Schools

The Woodwright's School & Tool Store
89A Hillsboro Street
Pittsboro, NC
www.woodwrightschool.com

Eastfield Village
East Nassau, NY
www.historiceastfield.org

Iron Hardware

Peter M. Ross, Blacksmith & Whitesmith
2232 White Smith Road
Siler City, NC 27344
rosspm@msn.com
919-663-3309

D. C. Mitchell
8 East Hadco Road
Wilmington, DE 19804
dave@dcmitchell.com
www.dcmitchell.org
302-998-1181

Bob Valentine
The Village Blacksmith Shop
221 North Street
Goshen, CT 06756
Bob@villageblacksmithshop.com
www.villageblacksmithshop.com
860-491-2371

House Movers

Wolfe House & Building Movers
10 Birch Lane
Bernville, PA 19506
www.wolfehousemovers.com
610-488-1020

Slate Countertops & Sinks

Sheldon Slate Products Company, Inc.
38 Farm Quarry Road
Monson, ME 04464
www.sheldonslate.com
207-997-3615

Paint Conservators

Building Conservation Associates
10 Langley Road
Newton Center, MA 02459
www.bcausa.com
617-916-5661

Wall Stencil & Mural Conservators

Center for Painted Wall Preservation
P. O. Box 187
Hallowell, ME 04347
www.pwpcenter.org

Window Restoration

The Window Preservation Alliance
www.windowpreservationalliance.org

Restoration Glass

Hollander Restoration Window Glass
www.restorationwindowglass.com

Wallpaper

Adelphi Paper Hangings
102 Main Street
P. O. Box 135
Sharon Springs, NY 13459
www.adelphipaperhangings.com
518-284-9066

Plasterer

Eugene Zordon & Sons
Torrington, CT 06790
860-601-5790

INDEX

Jim DeStefano is an engineer and architect and a Fellow of the Structural Engineering Institute. He is president of DeStefano & Chamberlain, which he founded in 1981 in Fairfield, Connecticut. Jim is a recognized authority on the restoration of historic structures and timber frame construction, and his projects have garnered numerous awards. He lives with his lovely wife, Vera, and their loyal mutts, Trixie and Jade, in an antique Connecticut home that he restored.